# Introduction: Stopping to Buy SparkNotes on a Snowy Evening

Whose words these are you *think* you know.
Your paper's due tomorrow, though;
We're glad to see you stopping here
To get some help before you go.

Lost your course? You'll find it here.
Face tests and essays without fear.
Between the words, good grades at stake:
Get great results throughout the year.

Once school bells caused your heart to quake
As teachers circled each mistake.
Use SparkNotes and no longer weep,
Ace every single test you take.

Yes, books are lovely, dark, and deep,
But only what you grasp you keep,
With hours to go before you sleep,
With hours to go before you sleep.

# THE JOY LUCK CLUB

*Amy Tan*

SPARKNOTES is a registered trademark of SparkNotes LLC.

Spark Publishing
A Division of Barnes & Noble
120 Fifth Avenue
New York, NY 10011
www.sparknotes.com

ISBN-13: 978-1-5866-3419-3
ISBN-10: 1-5866-3419-4

Please submit changes or report errors to www.sparknotes.com/errors.

Printed and bound in the United States

10

# Contents

# CONTEXT

AMY TAN WAS BORN in Oakland, California, in 1952. Her parents, both Chinese immigrants, lived in various towns in California before eventually settling in Santa Clara. When Tan was in her early teens, her father and one of her brothers each died of a brain tumor within months of each other. During this period, Tan learned that her mother had been married before, in China. Tan's mother had divorced her first husband, who had been abusive, and had fled China just before the Communist takeover in 1949. She left behind three daughters, whom she would not see again for nearly forty years.

After losing her husband and son, Tan's mother moved her family to Switzerland, where Tan finished high school. During these years, mother and daughter argued about Tan's college and career plans. Tan eventually followed her boyfriend to San Jose City College, where she earned a bachelor's and a master's degree in English and linguistics, despite her mother's wish that she study medicine.

After Tan married her boyfriend, Louis DeMattei, she began to pursue a Ph.D. in linguistics. She later abandoned the program in order to work with developmentally disabled children. Then she became a freelance business writer. Although she was successful, she found writing for corporate executives unfulfilling. She began to write fiction as a creative release.

Meanwhile, Tan's mother was suffering from a serious illness, and Tan resolved to take a trip to China with her mother if she recovered. In 1987, after her mother returned to health, they traveled to China, where Tan's mother was reunited with her daughters and Tan met her half-sisters. The trip provided Tan with a fresh perspective on her mother, and it served as the key inspiration for her first book, *The Joy Luck Club*. Soon after its publication in 1989, *The Joy Luck Club* garnered enthusiastic reviews, remaining on the *New York Times* bestseller list for many months. It won both the National Book Award and the *L.A. Times* Book Award in 1989.

Tan continues to publish popular works. In response to the widely held opinion that she writes with a social aim—to portray the Chinese American experience—Tan often emphasizes that she writes first and foremost as an artist. She argues that her bicultural upbringing is her work's source of inspiration but not its primary subject. Through her writing, Tan approaches issues that are universally applicable to all groups of people. She explores themes of family and memory, as well as the conflicts of culture that arise in so many American communities.

# PLOT OVERVIEW

THE JOY LUCK CLUB contains sixteen interwoven stories about conflicts between Chinese immigrant mothers and their American-raised daughters. The book hinges on Jing-mei's trip to China to meet her half-sisters, twins Chwun Yu and Chwun Hwa. The half-sisters remained behind in China because Jing-mei's mother, Suyuan, was forced to leave them on the roadside during her desperate flight from Japan's invasion of Kweilin during World War II. Jing-mei was born to a different father years later, in America. Suyuan intended to return to China for her other daughters, but failed to find them before her death.

Jing-mei has taken her mother's place playing mahjong in a weekly gathering her mother had organized in China and revived in San Francisco: the Joy Luck Club. The club's other members—Lindo, Ying-ying, and An-mei—are three of her mother's oldest friends and fellow immigrants. They tell Jing-mei that just before Suyuan died, she had finally succeeded in locating the address of her lost daughters. The three women repeatedly urge Jing-mei to travel to China and tell her sisters about their mother's life. But Jing-mei wonders whether she is capable of telling her mother's story, and the three older women fear that Jing-mei's doubts may be justified. They fear that their own daughters, like Jing-mei, may not know or appreciate the stories of their mothers' lives.

The novel is composed of four sections, each of which contains four separate narratives. In the first four stories of the book, the mothers, speaking in turn, recall with astonishing clarity their relationships with their own mothers, and they worry that their daughters' recollections of them will never possess the same intensity. In the second section, these daughters—Waverly, Jing-mei, Lena, and Rose—relate their recollections of their childhood relationships with their mothers; the great lucidity and force with which they tell their stories proves their mothers' fears at least partially unfounded. In the third group of stories, the four daughters narrate their adult dilemmas—troubles in marriage and with their careers. Although they believe that their mothers' antiquated ideas do not pertain to their own very American lifestyles, their search for solutions inevitably brings them back to their relationships with the older generation. In the final group of stories, the mothers struggle to offer solutions and support to their daughters, in the process learning more about themselves. Lindo recognizes through her daughter Waverly that she has been irrevocably changed by American culture. Ying-ying realizes that Lena has unwittingly followed her passive example in her marriage to Harold Livotny. An-mei realizes that Rose has not completely understood the lessons she intended to teach her about faith and hope.

Although Jing-mei fears that she cannot adequately portray her mother's life, Suyuan's story permeates the novel via Jing-mei's voice: she speaks for Suyuan in the first and fourth sections, the two "mothers' sections," of the novel. Suyuan's story is representative of the struggle to maintain the mother-daughter bond across cultural and generational gaps; by telling this story as her mother's daughter, Jing-mei enacts and cements the very bond that is the subject of Suyuan's story. When Jing-mei finally travels to China and helps her half-sisters to know a mother they cannot remember, she forges two other mother-daughter bonds as well. Her journey represents a reconciliation between Suyuan's two lives, between two cultures, and between mother and daughter. This enables Jing-mei to bring closure and resolution to her mother's story, but also to her own. In addition, the journey brings hope to the other members of the Joy Luck Club that they too can reconcile the oppositions in their lives between past and present, between cultures, and between generations.

# CHARACTER LIST

*The character list is divided into four sections, according to the mother-daughter pairs who narrate* THE JOY LUCK CLUB'*s sixteen stories. Each family's list includes family members along with other characters associated with the family or who appear exclusively in the family's stories.*

## WOO FAMILY

*Jing-mei (June) Woo* Jing-mei Woo is the newest member of the Joy Luck Club, having taken her mother Suyuan's place after her death. The other members of the Joy Luck Club give her money to travel to China so that she can find her mother's long-lost twin daughters, Chwun Yu and Chwun Hwa, and tell them Suyuan's story, but Jing-mei fears that she is not up to the task. See "Analysis of Major Characters."

*Suyuan Woo* Suyuan Woo was Jing-mei's mother and the founder of the Joy Luck Club, a group of women who come together once weekly to play mahjong. She started the club in China, in the early days of her first marriage. During her flight from a war-torn area of China, Suyuan lost her twin daughters, Chwun Yu and Chwun Hwa. In San Francisco, Suyuan revived the Joy Luck Club with Lindo, An-mei, and Ying-ying. See "Analysis of Major Characters."

*Canning Woo* Canning Woo is Suyuan's second husband and father of her daughter Jing-mei. He met Suyuan in the hospital in Chungking, where she recovered from her flight from Kweilin. After Suyuan's death, he travels to China with Jing-mei to meet her children.

*Wang Chwun Yu and Wang Chwun HwaChwun* Yu and Chwun Hwa are Suyuan's twin daughters by her first husband, Wang Fuchi; they are the half-sisters of Jing-mei. When an officer warned Suyuan to go to Chungking with her daughters to be with Wang Fuchi, Suyuan knew the Japanese were going to invade Kweilin. After many hardships and the onset of dysentery, Suyuan was forced to leave the twins by the side of the road, but Jing-mei and Canning are reunited with them at the end of the novel and tell them their mother's story.

## JONG FAMILY

*Lindo Jong* Lindo is a member of the Joy Luck Club. She teaches the power of invisible strength to her daughter Waverly, instilling in her the skills that contribute to Waverly's talent in chess. She fears that in trying to give Waverly American opportunities, she may have undermined her daughter's Chinese identity; Lindo also fears that she herself may have become too assimilated. See "Analysis of Major Characters."

*Waverly Jong* Waverly is the youngest of Lindo and Tin Jong's children. She has always been a model of success, winning chess tournaments as a child and eventually building a lucrative career as an attorney. Jing-mei has always felt a rivalry with her, somewhat imposed by their competitive mothers. Much of Waverly's talent in chess stemmed from her ability to hide her thoughts and channel invisible powers. Waverly fears what her mother will say about her white fiancé, Rich. See "Analysis of Major Characters."

*Tin Jong* Tin is Lindo's second husband. He is the father of her three children: Vincent, Waverly, and Winston.

*Vincent Jong* Vincent is Lindo and Tin Jong's second child. When he received a secondhand chess set at a church-sponsored Christmas party, his sister Waverly discovered her interest and talent in chess.

*Winston Jong* Winston was Lindo and Tin Jong first child. He was killed in a car accident at the age of sixteen.

*Huang Tyan-yu* Tyan-yu was Lindo Jong's first husband, in China. His mother was Huang Taitai. When Tyan-yu and Lindo were one and two, respectively, a matchmaker arranged for their marriage. Pampered and self-centered, Tyan-yu makes Lindo's life extremely unpleasant when she comes to live with his family at the age of twelve. When Lindo is sixteen, they get married, but Tyan-yu remains very much a boy. He has no desire for Lindo, but he is too afraid to admit it.

*Huang Taitai* Huang Taitai was Tyan-yu's mother. When Lindo came to live in her household at the age of twelve, Taitai trained her to be the epitome of the obedient wife. Domineering and tyrannical, Taitai made Lindo's life miserable and ignorantly blamed her for the fact that Lindo and Tyan-yu had no children.

*Marvin Chen* Marvin was Waverly's first husband and is the father of her daughter, Shoshana. Waverly's mother Lindo was very critical of Marvin, always pointing out his faults. Soon Waverly could see nothing but his shortcomings, and consequently divorced him. Waverly fears that the same thing will happen when she marries Rich.

*Shoshana Chen* Shoshana is Waverly's four-year-old daughter. Waverly's unconditional love for Shoshana teaches her about maternal devotion.

*Lindo's mother* After Lindo was engaged at the age of two, Lindo's mother began to talk about Lindo as if she were already her mother-in-law Huang Taitai's daughter. Lindo knows that her mother did so only because she wanted to keep herself from feeling too attached to the daughter she loved so dearly but had already given away.

*Rich Schields* Schields is Waverly's white fiancé. Waverly wants to tell her mother Lindo about their engagement, but she is afraid that Lindo will criticize him to the point that she will be unable to see anything but his faults. Rich loves Waverly unconditionally, but Waverly fears that a bad first impression will unleash a flood of criticism from Lindo.

## HSU FAMILY

*An-mei Hsu* An-mei is one of the members of the Joy Luck Club. She has learned important lessons about the dangers of passivity and the necessity of speaking up for herself, but, she notes with pain, she has not passed on these lessons to her daughter Rose. Although she has lost most of her faith in God, An-mei maintains a certain faith in the human power of will and effort. See "Analysis of Major Characters."

*Rose Hsu* Rose is the youngest of An-mei and George Hsu's three daughters. She married Ted Jordan, despite protests from both An-mei and Mrs. Jordan. She has always allowed Ted to make all the decisions, but when Ted asks her to take on some of the responsibility, Rose's relationship with Ted disintegrates. An-mei helps Rose understand that she needs to assert herself. See "Analysis of Major Characters."

*Bing Hsu*  Bing was the youngest of An-mei's and George Hsu's seven children. When Bing was four years old, the entire Hsu family took a trip to the beach, and Bing drowned. Rose, rather irrationally, blames herself for the death. An-mei had faith that God and her *nengkan,* or her belief in her power to control her fate, would help her find Bing, but the boy never turned up.

*George Hsu* George is An-mei's husband and Rose's father.

*An-mei's mother* An-mei's mother was a strong but sorrowful woman who, after being widowed while still young, was tricked into becoming the fourth wife of Wu Tsing. She went to live in his household in the city of Tientsin. When An-mei's grandmother, Popo, dies, An-mei goes to live with her mother in the city. Eventually, An-mei's mother commits suicide so that An-mei will not live a life of shame and unhappiness. An-mei's mother teaches her daughter to sacrifice herself for her family, to swallow her tears, to mask her pain, and to beware of people who seem too kind or generous.

*Popo*  Popo was An-mei's maternal grandmother. When An-mei's mother married Wu Tsing, Popo disowned her. According to traditional Chinese values, it was a disgrace that her widowed daughter had not only remarried but had re-married as a third concubine. Five years after leaving, An-mei's mother returned because Popo had fallen terminally ill and, according to superstitious healing methods, sliced off a piece of her flesh to put in a broth for Popo.

*Wu Tsing*  Wu Tsing was a wealthy Chinese merchant who took An-mei's mother as his third concubine, or "Fourth Wife." He was easily manipulated by Second Wife and was, at root, a coward. When An-mei's mother commits suicide, he fears the vengeance of her ghost and thus promises to raise An-mei in wealth and status.

CHARACTER LIST

*Second Wife* Second Wife was Wu Tsing's first concubine. She entirely dominates the household in Tientsin, providing an example of extreme female power in a patriarchal society. Yet hers is a cruel power: she is deceptive and manipulative. She banks on her husband's fear of ghosts by faking suicides so that he will give her what she wants, and she trapped An-mei's mother into marrying Wu Tsing so as to fulfill his wish for heirs without losing her authority. At first, Second Wife manipulates An-mei into liking her by giving her a pearl necklace, but An-mei's mother shows An-mei the deceptiveness of appearances by shattering one of the "pearls" with her foot in order to prove that it is actually glass. An-mei repeats this action after her mother's suicide, and Second Wife is the first figure against whom An-mei learns to assert her own strength.

*Syaudi* Syaudi was the son of An-mei's mother and her second husband, Wu-Tsing, but Second Wife took him as her own. An-mei learned that he was her brother through Yan Chang, her mother's servant.

*Ted Jordan* Ted Jordan is Rose's estranged husband. When they were dating, he made all the decisions. Later, he asks for a divorce and is surprised when Rose stands up for herself.

## St. Clair Family

*Ying-ying St. Clair* Ying-ying is a member of the Joy Luck Club. As a child, Ying-ying was headstrong and independent. Yet she slowly develops a fatalism and passivity; rarely speaking her mind, she allows her American husband, Clifford St. Clair, to translate incorrectly her feelings and thoughts. Once she realizes that her daughter Lena exhibits the same qualities in her own marriage, Ying-ying recognizes her weakness and resolves to tell Lena her story. See "Analysis of Major Characters."

*Lena St. Clair* Lena is the only child of Ying-ying and Clifford St. Clair. When she married Harold Livotny, Lena unwittingly began to follow Ying-ying's passive example, believing herself incapable of control in her marriage and her career. See "Analysis of Major Characters."

*Clifford St. Clair* Clifford St. Clair is Ying-ying's second husband. He never learned to speak Chinese fluently, and she never learned to speak English fluently. Clifford often puts words into his wife's mouth.

*Ying-ying's Amah* Ying-ying's Amah was her childhood nursemaid. She loved Ying-ying as if she were her own child and tried to instill traditional Chinese feminine values in her—values that Ying-ying will later regret having adopted.

*Harold Livotny* Harold is Lena St. Clair's husband. Since the beginning of their relationship, he has insisted that they split the cost of everything they share. He says that keeping their finances separate makes their love purer. However, what he believes will keep them independent and equal in fact renders Lena rather powerless.

# ANALYSIS OF MAJOR CHARACTERS

## JING-MEI (JUNE) WOO

In a way, Jing-mei Woo is the main character of *The Joy Luck Club*. Structurally, her narratives serve as bridges between the two generations of storytellers, as Jing-mei speaks both for herself and for her recently deceased mother, Suyuan. Jing-mei also bridges America and China. When she travels to China, she discovers the Chinese essence within herself, thus realizing a deep connection to her mother that she had always ignored. She also brings Suyuan's story to her long-lost twin daughters, and, once reunited with her half-sisters, gains an even more profound understanding of who her mother was.

For the most part, Jing-mei's fears echo those of her peers, the other daughters of the Joy Luck Club members. They have always identified with Americans (Jing-mei also goes by the English name "June") but are beginning to regret having neglected their Chinese heritage. Her fears also speak to a reciprocal fear shared by the mothers, who wonder whether, by giving their daughters American opportunities and self-sufficiency, they have alienated them from their Chinese heritage.

Jing-mei is representative in other ways as well. She believes that her mother's constant criticism bespeaks a lack of affection, when in fact her mother's severity and high expectations are expressions of love and faith in her daughter. All of the other mother-daughter pairs experience the same misunderstanding, which in some ways may be seen to stem from cultural differences. What Tan portrays as the traditional Chinese values of filial obedience, criticism-enveloped expressions of love, and the concealment of excessive emotions all clash with the daughters' "American" ideas about autonomy, free and open speech, and self-esteem. However, by eventually creating a bridge between China and America, between mothers and daughters, Jing-mei ultimately reconciles some of these cultural and generational differences, providing hope for the other mother-daughter pairs.

## SUYUAN WOO

Suyuan Woo is a strong and willful woman who refuses to focus on her hardships. Instead, she struggles to create happiness and success where she finds it lacking. It is with this mentality that she founds the original Joy Luck Club while awaiting the Japanese invasion of China in Kweilin. Her sense of the power of will can at times cause problems, such as when Suyuan believes that her daughter Jing-mei can be a child prodigy if only the Woos can locate her talent and nurture it well enough. This leads to a deep resentment in Jing-mei. Yet it is also by virtue of Suyuan's will that she eventually locates her long-lost twin daughters in China. Only her death prevents her from returning to them.

Suyuan shares many characteristics with her fellow mothers in the Joy Luck Club: fierce love for her daughter, often expressed as criticism; a distress at her daughter's desire to shake off her Chinese identity in favor of an American one; and a fear that she may be alienated from her daughter either because of her own actions or because of their divergent ages and cultural upbringings.

## AN-MEI HSU

At an early age, An-mei Hsu learns lessons in stoic and severe love from her grandmother, Popo, and from her mother. Her mother also teaches her to swallow her tears, to conceal her pain, and to distrust others. Although An-mei later learns to speak up and assert herself, she fears that she has handed down a certain passivity to her daughter Rose.

An-mei sees "fate" as what one is "destined" to struggle toward achieving. When her youngest child Bing dies, An-mei ceases to express any outward faith in God, but retains her belief in the force of will. Rose initially believed that the death had caused her mother to lose faith altogether, but she eventually realizes that she may have misinterpreted her mother's behaviors.

## ROSE HSU JORDAN

Rose Hsu Jordan finds herself unable to assert her opinion, to stand up for herself, or to make decisions. Although she once displayed a certain strength, illustrated by her insistence on marrying her husband, Ted, despite her mother's objections and her mother-in-law's poorly concealed racism, she has allowed herself to become the "victim" to Ted's "hero," letting him make all of the decisions in their life together. She finally needs her mother's intervention in order to realize that to refuse to make decisions is in fact itself a decision: a decision to continue in a state of subservience, inferiority, and ultimate unhappiness.

Rose's youngest brother, Bing, died when he was four years old. Because Bing drowned at the beach while Rose was supposed to be watching him, Rose feels responsible for his death, despite the fact that the rest of the family does not hold Rose accountable. Her refusal to take on future responsibilities may stem from her fear of future blame should misfortunes occur.

## LINDO JONG

Lindo Jong learns from an early age the powers of "invisible strength"—of hiding one's thoughts until the time is ripe to reveal them, and of believing in one's inner force even when one finds oneself at a disadvantage. She discovers these values while in China, caught in a loveless marriage and oppressed by the tyranny of her mother-in-law. By playing upon her mother-in-law's superstition and fear, Lindo eventually extricates herself from the marriage with her dignity intact, and without dishonoring her parents' promise to her husband's family.

Lindo later teaches these skills of invisible strength—for which she uses the wind as a metaphor—to her daughter Waverly. Her lessons nurture Waverly's skill at chess, but Waverly comes to resent her mother's control and seeming claims of ownership over her successes. Eventually, Waverly seems to become ashamed of Lindo and misunderstands her as a critical, controlling, and narrow-minded old woman.

Lindo perhaps experiences the largest crisis of cultural identity of any of the characters. She regrets having wanted to give Waverly both American circumstances and a Chinese character, stating that the two can never successfully combine. She thinks that from the moment she gave Waverly an American name—she named her after the street where the family lived—she has allowed her daughter to become too American, and consequently contributed to the barrier that separates them. At the same time, however, she recognizes her own American characteristics and knows that she is no longer "fully Chinese": during her recent visit to China, people recognized her as a tourist. Distressed by this, Lindo wonders what she has lost by the alteration. Her strategies of concealing inner powers and knowledge may be related to her ability to maintain what Waverly characterizes as a type of "two-facedness"—an ability to switch between a "Chinese" and an "American" face depending on whom she is with.

## WAVERLY JONG

From her mother, Waverly inherits her "invisible strength"—her ability to conceal her thoughts and strategize. Although she applies these to chess as a child, she later turns them on her mother, Lindo, as well, imagining her struggles with her mother as a tournament.

Waverly's focus on invisible strength also contributes to a sense of competitiveness: she feels a rivalry with Jing-mei and humiliates her in front of the others at Suyuan's New Year's dinner. Yet Waverly is not entirely self-centered: she loves her daughter, Shoshana, unconditionally. Nor is she without insecurities: she fears her mother's criticism of her fiancé, Rich. In fact, it seems that Waverly tends to project her fears and dislikes onto her mother. As she sits through dinner with her parents and Rich, she becomes distraught as she imagines her mother's growing hatred of her fiancé. Yet, later on, she realizes that her mother in fact likes Rich—Waverly was the one with the misgivings, perhaps a sort of cultural guilt: Rich is white, and Waverly does not like to think that she has lost her ties to her Chinese heritage.

## YING-YING ST. CLAIR

Ying-ying was born in the year of the Tiger, a creature of force and stealth. However, when her nursemaid tells her that girls should be meek and passive, Ying-ying begins to lose her sense of autonomous will. Furthermore, at an early age Ying-ying's profound belief in fate and her personal destiny led to a policy of passivity and even listlessness. Always listening to omens and signs, she never paid attention to her inner feelings. Because she believed that she was "destined" to marry a vulgar family friend, she did nothing to seriously prevent the marriage, and even came to love her husband, as if against her will. When he died, she allowed the American Clifford St. Clair to marry her because she sensed that he was her destiny as well. For years she let Clifford mistranslate her clipped sentences, her gestures, and her silences.

CHARACTER ANALYSIS

Only after Ying-ying realizes that she has passed on her passivity and fatalism to her daughter Lena does she take any initiative to change. Seeing her daughter in an unhappy marriage, she urges her to take control. She tells Lena her story for the first time, hoping that she might learn from her mother's own failure to take initiative and instead come to express her thoughts and feelings. Lena, too, was born in the year of the Tiger, and Ying-ying hopes that her daughter can live up to their common horoscope in a way that she herself failed to do. Moreover, in this belief in astrology Ying-ying finds a sort of positive counterpart to her earlier, debilitating superstitions and fatalism, for it is a belief not in the inevitability of external events but in the power of an internal quality.

## LENA ST. CLAIR

Lena St. Clair is caught in an unhappy marriage to Harold Livotny. Harold insists that the couple keep separate bank accounts and use a balance sheet to detail their monetary debts to one another. Although he believes that this policy will keep money out of the relationship, it in fact accomplishes the opposite, making money and obligation central to Lena and Harold's conjugal life. Lena has inherited her mother Ying-ying's belief in superstition and deems herself incapable of reversing what is "fated" to happen. She fails to take initiative to change her relationship, despite her recognition of its dysfunctional elements.

While still a child, Lena learns an important lesson from her neighbors. She constantly hears the mother and daughter in the adjacent apartment yelling, fighting, and even throwing things. She is shocked by the difference between these noisy confrontations and her own relationship with her mother, which is marked by silences and avoidance of conflict. Yet, when she realizes that the shouting and weeping she hears through the wall in fact express a kind of deep love between mother and daughter, she realizes the importance of expressing one's feelings, even at the cost of peace and harmony. Although the neighboring family lives a life of conflict and sometimes even chaos, they possess a certainty of their love for each other that Lena feels to be lacking in her own home. Reflecting back on this episode of her life, Lena begins to realize how she might apply the lesson she learned then to her married life with Harold.

# THEMES, MOTIFS & SYMBOLS

## THEMES

*Themes are the fundamental and often universal ideas explored in a literary work.*

### THE CHALLENGES OF CULTURAL TRANSLATION

Throughout *The Joy Luck Club,* the various narrators meditate on their inability to translate concepts and sentiments from one culture to another. The incomplete cultural understanding of both the mothers and the daughters owes to their incomplete knowledge of language. Additionally, the barriers that exist *between* the mothers and the daughters are often due to their inability to communicate with one another. Although the daughters know some Chinese words and the mothers speak some English, communication often becomes a matter of translation, of words whose intended meaning and accepted meaning are in fact quite separate, leading to subtle misunderstandings.

The first mention of this difficulty with translation occurs when Jing-mei relates the story of her mother's founding of the Joy Luck Club. After attempting to explain the significance of the club's name, Jing-mei recognizes that the concept is not something that can be translated. She points out that the daughters think their mothers are stupid because of their fractured English, while the mothers are impatient with their daughters who don't understand the cultural nuances of their language and who do not intend to pass along their Chinese heritage to their own children. Throughout the book, characters bring up one Chinese concept after another, only to accept the frustrating fact that an understanding of Chinese culture is a prerequisite to understanding its meaning.

### THE POWER OF STORYTELLING

Because the barriers between the Chinese and the American cultures are exacerbated by imperfect translation of language, the mothers use storytelling to circumvent these barriers and communicate with their daughters. The stories they tell are often educational, warning against certain mistakes or giving advice based on past successes. For instance, Ying-ying's decision to tell Lena about her past is motivated by her desire to warn Lena against the passivity and fatalism that Ying-ying suffered. Storytelling is also employed to communicate messages of love and pride, and to illumine one's inner self for others.

Another use of storytelling concerns historical legacy. By telling their daughters about their family histories, the mothers ensure that their lives are remembered and understood by subsequent generations, so that the characters who acted in the story never die away completely. In telling their stories to their daughters, the mothers try to instill them with respect for their Chinese ancestors and their Chinese pasts. Suyuan hopes that by finding her long-lost daughters and telling them her story, she can assure them of her love, despite her apparent abandonment of them. When Jing-mei sets out to tell her half-sisters Suyuan's story, she also has this goal in mind, as well as her own goal of letting the twins know who their mother was and what she was like.

Storytelling is also used as a way of controlling one's own fate. In many ways, the original purpose of the Joy Luck Club was to create a place to exchange stories. Faced with pain and hardship, Suyuan decided to take control of the plot of her life. The Joy Luck Club did not simply serve as a distraction; it also enabled transformation—of community, of love and support, of circumstance. Stories work to encourage a certain sense of independence. They are a way of forging one's own identity and gaining autonomy. Waverly understands this: while Lindo believes that her daughter's crooked nose means that she is ill-fated, Waverly dismisses this passive interpretation and changes her identity and her fate by reinventing the story that is told about a crooked nose.

## THE PROBLEM OF IMMIGRANT IDENTITY

At some point in the novel, each of the major characters expresses anxiety over her inability to reconcile her Chinese heritage with her American surroundings. Indeed, this reconciliation is the very aim of Jing-mei's journey to China. While the daughters in the novel are genetically Chinese (except for Lena, who is half Chinese) and have been raised in mostly Chinese households, they also identify with and feel at home in modern American culture. Waverly, Rose, and Lena all have white boyfriends or husbands, and they regard many of their mothers' customs and tastes as old-fashioned or even ridiculous. Most of them have spent their childhoods trying to escape their Chinese identities: Lena would walk around the house with her eyes opened as far as possible so as to make them look European. Jing-mei denied during adolescence that she had any internal Chinese aspects, insisting that her Chinese identity was limited only to her external features. Lindo meditates that Waverly would have clapped her hands for joy during her teen years if her mother had told her that she did not look Chinese.

As they mature, the daughters begin to sense that their identities are incomplete and become interested in their Chinese heritage. Waverly speaks wishfully about blending in too well in China and becomes angry when Lindo notes that she will be recognized instantly as a tourist. One of Jing-mei's greatest fears about her trip to China is not that others will recognize her as American, but that she herself will fail to recognize any Chinese elements within herself.

Of the four mothers, Lindo expresses the most anxiety over her cultural identity. Having been spotted as a tourist during her recent trip to China, she wonders how America has changed her. She has always believed in her ability to shift between her true self and her public self, but she begins to wonder whether her "true" self is not, in fact, her American one. Even while a young girl in China, Lindo showed that she did not completely agree with Chinese custom. She agonized over how to extricate herself from a miserable marriage without dishonoring her parents' promise to her husband's family. While her concern for her parents shows that Lindo did not wish to openly rebel against her tradition, Lindo made a secret promise to herself to remain true to her own desires. This promise shows the value she places on autonomy and personal happiness—two qualities that Lindo associates with American culture.

Jing-mei's experience in China at the end of the book certainly seems to support the possibility of a richly mixed identity rather than an identity of warring opposites. She comes to see that China itself contains American aspects, just as the part of America she grew up in—San Francisco's Chinatown—contained Chinese elements. Thus, her first meal in China consists of hamburgers and apple pie, per the request of her fully "Chinese" relatives. Perhaps, then, there is no such thing as a pure state of being Chinese, a pure state of being American; all individuals are amalgams of their unique tastes, habits, hopes, and memories. For immigrants and their families, the contrasts within this amalgam can bring particular pain as well as particular richness.

## MOTIFS

*Motifs are recurring structures, contrasts, or literary devices that can help to develop and inform the text's major themes.*

### CONTROL OVER ONE'S DESTINY

*The Joy Luck Club* contains an ongoing discussion about the extent to which characters have power over their own destinies. Elements from the Chinese belief system—the twelve animals of the zodiac, the five elements—reappear in the characters' explanations of their personalities. For example, Ying-ying St. Clair speaks about how she and her daughter, Lena, are both Tigers, according to the years in which they were born. The "black" side of her Tiger personality is that she waits, like a predator, for the right moment for the "gold" side to act—the right moment to snatch what she wants. Yet Ying-ying's behavior contradicts this symbolic explanation of her character. Ironically, her belief in "fate" ends up negating her understanding of her "fated" nature. She believes she is destined to marry a certain vulgar older man in China, does so, and then ends up feeling bereft after she learns of his infidelity. She shows she can take matters into her own hands when she aborts the fetus of the unborn child from her first marriage, but then falls back into the same trap when she "allows" Lena's father, Clifford, to marry her because she thinks it is her destiny. She lives in constant anxiety and fear from tragedies that she believes she is powerless to prevent.

Jing-mei and her mother also clash because of their opposing concepts of destiny. Suyuan believes that Jing-mei will manifest an inner prodigy if only she and her daughter work hard enough to discover and cultivate Jing-mei's talent. Jing-mei, on the other hand, believes that there are ultimately things about her that cannot be forced; she is who she is.

An-mei Hsu seems to possess a notion of a balance between fate and will. She believes strongly in the will, and yet she also sees this will as somehow "fated." While her faith in her ability to will her own desires becomes less explicitly religious after the loss of her son Bing, An-mei never resigned herself, as Ying-ying does, to thinking that human beings have no control over what happens to them. Thus, when Rose asks why she should try to save her marriage, saying there is no hope, no reason to try, An-mei responds that she should try simply because she "must." "This is your fate," she says, "what you must do." Rose comes to realize that for her mother, the powers of "fate" and "faith" are co-dependent rather than mutually exclusive.

## SEXISM

Sexism is a problem common to both Chinese and American cultures, and as such they are encountered by most of the characters in the novel. In China, for example, Lindo is forced to live almost as a servant to her mother-in-law and husband, conforming to idealized roles of feminine submission and duty. Because An-mei's mother is raped by her future husband, she must marry him to preserve her honor; whereas he, as a man, may marry any number of concubines without being judged harshly. Indeed, it is considered shameful for An-mei's mother to marry at all after her first husband's death, to say nothing of her becoming a concubine, and An-mei's mother is disowned by her mother (Popo) because of the rigid notions of purity and virtue held by the patriarchal Chinese society. Ying-ying's nursemaid tells her that girls should never ask but only listen, thus conveying her society's sexist standards for women and instilling in Ying-ying a tragic passivity.

In America, the daughters also encounter sexism as they grow up. Waverly experiences resistance when she asks to play chess with the older men in the park in Chinatown: they tell her they do not want to play with dolls and express surprise at her skill in a game at which men excel. Rose's passivity with Ted is based on the stereotypical gender roles of a proactive, heroic male and a submissive, victimized female. Lena's agreement to serve as a mere associate in the architecture firm that she helped her husband to found, as well as her agreement to make a fraction of his salary, may also be based on sexist assumptions that she has absorbed. Tan seems to make the distinction between a respect for tradition and a disrespect for oneself as an individual. Submission to sexist modes of thought and behavior, regardless of cultural tradition, seems to be unacceptable as it encompasses a passive destruction of one's autonomy.

## SACRIFICES FOR LOVE

Many of the characters make great sacrifices for the love of their children or parents. The selflessness of their devotion speaks to the force of the bond between parent and child. An-mei's mother slices off a piece of her own flesh to put in her mother's soup, hoping superstitiously to cure her. An-mei's mother's later suicide could also be seen not as an act of selfish desperation but as one of selfless sacrifice to her daughter's future happiness: because Wu-Tsing is afraid of ghosts, An-mei's mother knows that in death she can ensure her daughter's continued status and comfort in the household with more certainty than she could in life. Later, An-mei throws her one memento of her mother, her sapphire ring, into the waves in hopes of placating the evil spirits that have taken her son Bing. So, too, does Suyuan take an extra job cleaning the house of a family with a piano, in order to earn Jing-mei the opportunity to practice the instrument. These acts of sacrifice speak to the power of the mother-daughter bond. Despite being repeatedly weakened—or at least tested—by cultural, linguistic, and generational gulfs, the sacrifices the characters make prove that this bond is not in danger of being destroyed.

# SYMBOLS

*Symbols are objects, characters, figures, or colors used to represent abstract ideas or concepts.*

## SUYUAN'S PENDANT

In Jing-mei's story "Best Quality," she discusses the jade pendant her mother, Suyuan, gave her, which she called her "life's importance." Over the course of the story, the symbolic meaning of the pendant changes. At first, Jing-mei found the pendant garish and unstylish; to her it represented the cultural differences between herself and her mother. After Suyuan's death, however, Jing-mei comes to see it as a symbol of her mother's love and concern. It is particularly interesting to note that, in its very ability to change meanings, the pendant gains an additional symbolism: it symbolizes the human power to assign new meanings to the phenomena around us. The development that Jing-mei undergoes in understanding the gift of the pendant symbolizes her development in understanding her mother's gestures in general. While Jing-mei used to interpret many of her mother's words as expressions of superstition or criticism, she now sees them as manifesting a deep maternal wisdom and love.

## LENA'S VASE

In the story "Rice Husband," a vase in Lena's home comes to symbolize her marriage. Lena had placed the vase upon a wobbly table; she knew the placement of the vase there was dangerous, but she did nothing to protect the vase from breaking. Like the vase, Lena's marriage is in danger of falling and shattering. According to the text, it was Lena's husband, Harold, who built the wobbly table when he was first studying architecture and design. If one takes this information as similarly symbolic, one might say that the precariousness of the marriage may result from Harold's failure to be "supportive" enough, "solid" enough in his commitment. In any case, Lena, too, is to blame: as with the vase, Lena realizes that her marriage is in danger of shattering, but she refuses to take action. When Ying-ying "accidentally" causes the vase to break on the floor, she lets Lena know that she should prevent disasters before they happen, rather than stand by passively as Ying-ying herself has done throughout her life.

## LINDO'S RED CANDLE

When Lindo Jong is married, she and her husband light a red candle with a wick at each end. The name of the bride is marked at one end of the candle, and the name of the groom at the other. If the candle burns all night without either end extinguishing prematurely, custom says that the marriage will be successful and happy. The candle has a symbolic meaning—the success of the marriage—within the Chinese culture, but within the story it also functions as a symbol of traditional Chinese culture itself: it embodies the ancient beliefs and customs surrounding marriage.

Lindo feels conflicted about her marriage: she desperately does not want to enter into the subservience she knows the wedding will bring, yet she cannot go against the promises her parents made to her husband's family. In order to free herself from the dilemma, she secretly blows out her husband's side of the candle. A servant relights it, but Lindo later reveals to her mother-in-law that the flame went out, implying that it did so without human intervention. By blowing out the flame, Lindo takes control of her own fate, eventually extricating herself from an unhappy marriage. Thus, the candle also symbolizes her self-assertion and control over her own life.

It is important to consider the candle's original symbolism as a sign of tradition and culture, for it is by playing upon the traditional beliefs and superstitions that Lindo convinces her mother-in-law to annul the marriage. Her act of blowing out the candle would have been meaningless without an underlying, pre-established network of belief. Thus the candle, first a symbol of tradition, then of self-assertion, ultimately comes to symbolize the use of tradition in claiming one's own identity and power.

# SUMMARY & ANALYSIS

## FEATHERS FROM A THOUSAND LI AWAY: INTRODUCTION & "THE JOY LUCK CLUB"

### SUMMARY—INTRODUCTION

Each of the four sections of *The Joy Luck Club* is preceded by a short parable that introduces the major themes of that section's four stories. The parable that begins "Feathers from a Thousand *Li* Away" tells the tale of a Chinese woman who decides to emigrate to America. Before she leaves Shanghai, the woman buys a swan from a vendor, who tells her that the bird was once a duck. In an attempt to become a goose, the duck stretched its neck so far that it became a swan, exceeding its own hopes for itself. As the woman sails to America, she dreams of raising a daughter amid the plentiful opportunities of the new country. She imagines that her American-born daughter will resemble her in every way, except that, unlike her mother, she will be judged according to her own worth, not by that of a husband. Like the swan, the daughter will exceed all hopes, so the woman plans to give her daughter the swan as a gift. Yet, when the woman arrives in America, the immigration officials seize the swan and leave the woman with nothing but a feather. The daughter is born and grows up to be the strong, happy woman her mother had imagined. The woman still wishes to present the feather to her daughter and to explain its symbolic meaning, but for many years she holds back. She is still waiting "for the day she could [explain it] in perfect American English."

### SUMMARY—JING-MEI WOO: "THE JOY LUCK CLUB"

> *"What will I say? What can I tell them about my mother? I don't know anything...."*
>
> *(See* QUOTATIONS, *p. 69)*

Jing-mei opens her narrative by explaining that after her mother, Suyuan, died two months ago, her father, Canning, asked her to take her mother's place at the Joy Luck Club, a weekly mahjong party. (Mahjong is a game for four players involving dice and domino-like tiles.) Suyuan and Canning Woo have been attending the meetings of the Joy Luck Club since 1949, shortly after they emigrated from China to San Francisco. In fact, the San Francisco version of the club is a revival of the club Suyuan founded earlier, while she was still in China. Jing-mei tells her mother's story about the club's beginning.

Suyuan's first husband, Fuchi Wang, had been an officer in the Kuomintang, a militaristic, nationalist political party that ran China from 1928 through the 1940s. During the 1940s, the party's power was threatened by Japanese invasions and by the rising force of the Communists. Fuchi took Suyuan and their twin daughters, Chwun Yu and Chwun Hwa, to the town of Kweilin, leaving them there while he traveled to a city called Chungking. Kweilin was full of refugees at the time, and cultural, ethnic, and class tensions added to the hardships resulting from lack of food and money. During her stay in Kweilin, Suyuan created the Joy Luck Club with three other women in order to escape the fear and uncertainty of the war. They cooked "feasts," played mahjong, and traded stories into the night. "And [at each meeting], we could hope to be lucky," Suyuan told Jing- mei. "That hope was our only joy. And that's [why we called] . . . our little parties Joy Luck."

Jing-mei explains that usually her mother's story would stop at this point, and that her mother would tag on some fantastic ending that made the story seem like a "Chinese fairy tale." But one evening, her mother told her the story's real ending—the story about how she came to leave the original Joy Luck Club in Kweilin.

One day, an army officer suggested to Suyuan that she travel to Chungking to be with her husband. Suyuan knew the officer's message meant that the Japanese would soon arrive in Kweilin, and she knew that the families of officers would be the first to die. She packed her children and some belongings into a wheelbarrow and began to walk to Chungking. The journey was long, and Suyuan's hands began to bleed from carrying her bags. Finally she, like others before her, was forced to begin lightening her load by leaving items behind. By the time Suyuan arrived in Chungking, she had only three silk dresses. She made no mention of the babies. For years, she never told Jing-mei what happened to Jing-mei's older half-sisters.

At the Joy Luck Club meeting, Jing-mei cannot believe that she could ever really replace her mother. She remembers her mother's critical attitude toward everyone. Suyuan had always compared Jing-mei with her friend Lindo's daughter, Waverly. Jing-mei feels inadequate because she never succeeded in becoming the prize daughter that Waverly is, and she never finished college.

At her first Joy Luck Club event, Jing-mei suffers silently as the other members level veiled criticisms at her for having dropped out of school and having been evicted from her apartment. Just as she is about to leave, her mother's friends sit her down and inform her that they have some important news: Suyuan had been secretly searching for her twin daughters throughout her years in America, and just before her death, she had succeeded in locating their address. She died before she could contact them, however, so her friends decided to write a letter in her name. They have received a letter from Jing-mei's sisters in response. The Joy Luck members want Jing-mei to travel to China and tell her sisters about Suyuan's life; they give her $1,200 for the trip. Overwhelmed, Jing-mei cries and doubts whether she knew her mother well enough to tell the twins her story.

---

ANALYSIS—INTRODUCTION & "THE JOY LUCK CLUB"

The opening parable raises the issue of the linguistic and cultural barrier that exists between each immigrant mother and American-born daughter in the book. The daughter in the parable has never known the sorrows that her mother experienced in China, but she cannot appreciate her good fortune because she does not know her mother's story. Moreover, although the mother desires to live out her hopes through her daughter, the lack of communication between them prevents her wish from being granted in its entirety. Even if the mother were to learn "perfect American English," she would never be able to translate fully the nuances of her story. As the stories of The Joy Luck Club will demonstrate, such a process of translation all too often fails to convey the full meaning of a story: while individual words might have English equivalents, ultimately the Chinese and American cultures can never be equated. What the mother of the parable denotes as a language gap actually extends into many more aspects of life, and bridging the gap will entail more than simply learning extra vocabulary words. The characters in The Joy Luck Club will struggle to answer for themselves whether they can achieve the deeper level of communication necessary to achieve true understanding between cultures and generations.

Throughout The Joy Luck Club, issues of translation and story-telling emerge continually. The book explores the question of whether a story serves as a place where "losses in translation" become concentrated and magnified, or whether a story might function more like a stepping-stone or bridge, connecting mothers and daughters across the intergenerational and intercultural chasm that separates them.

When Suyuan came to the United States, she had lost almost everything: all she brought with her were three elaborate silk dresses. As a child, Jing-mei never appreciated the significance of those dresses, but to Suyuan, they testify to her survival and persist as her last material connection to her former life. In some ways, they are analogous to the single feather that the woman is left with in the section's introductory parable. Yet, even though she cherishes the dresses, Suyuan shows that she is able to focus not on what she has lost but on what she retains. She revives the Joy Luck Club with three new friends, and she raises her newborn daughter rather than mourning her lost twins. As she used to explain to Jing-mei about the original Joy Luck Club, "We all had our miseries. But . . . [w]hat was worse, we asked among ourselves, to sit and wait for our own deaths . . . ? Or to choose our own happiness?"

Suyuan repeatedly chooses her own happiness: by each time giving a different ending to the story about Kweilin and the original Joy Luck Club, she may be willfully creating this happiness. Perhaps, too, she hoped that she might some day find her daughters again, thus rendering the story's true ending the happiest of all. Until then, fairy-tale endings might substitute. A third possibility is that Suyuan omitted the tragedy from her story out of a belief that it would be impossible to make her American daughter, a child of comfortable and stable circumstances, understand the agonies she has known.

Indeed, Jing-mei herself fears that she does not know her mother well enough to tell her story to her half-sisters, Chwun Yu and Chwun Hwa. An-mei, Lindo, and Ying-ying, the other members of the club, react in horror when Jing-mei expresses her fear. Jing-mei believes that their dismay owes to their understanding that their children, too, lack knowledge of their mother's lives. They worry that their stories will be lost in the generational and cultural gap between themselves and their American daughters—just like the story of the mother in the parable.

The notion of this generational gap also feeds into Jing-mei's anxieties about replacing her mother in the club. To take her mother's place in the Joy Luck Club is to enact an important ritual, and to carry on the memory of what was begun in China and resurrected in America. It is to sustain a piece of her mother's past in her own present. Suyuan created the Joy Luck Club in Kweilin because she wanted to reaffirm, or create, a sense of gladness, belonging, and order, even in the midst of complete uncertainty and turmoil. In America, the club has served a similar purpose, and also helped Suyuan and the other members feel a sense of continuity between their old and new cultures. For Suyuan, the club was a symbol of hope and of strength, and a means of asserting identity amidst change. Jing-mei wonders whether she can uphold her mother's memory and identity, whether she is strong enough to carry her mother's hopes into the future. Jing-mei's guilty remarks about not having met her mother's expectations that she would finish college and find a well-paying career suggest that she fears that, in some way, she already represents the failure of Suyuan's dreams.

# FEATHERS FROM A THOUSAND LI AWAY: "SCAR," "THE RED CANDLE," & "THE MOON LADY"

### SUMMARY—AN-MEI HSU: "SCAR"

An-mei's mother became the concubine of a man named Wu-Tsing when An-mei was four, so she and her little brother went to live with their grandmother, Popo, who forbade them to speak their mother's name. After a few years, An-mei forgot her mother entirely.

When Popo became terminally ill, An-mei's mother visited for the first time in five years. As she brushed An-mei's hair and caressed a scar on her neck, An-mei's memory came rushing back; she remembers that when she was four, her mother arrived at Popo's house to beg her to give An-mei back. An-mei cried out for her mother, and a bowl of boiling soup spilled over her neck like a flood of boiling anger. Popo and the rest of the family chased An-mei's mother away, and after a while, the burn wound turned into a scar.

Later, just before Popo died, An-mei saw her mother cut a piece of her own flesh out of her arm and put it in a soup for Popo. According to ancient tradition, such a sacrifice might cure a dying family member. It is also a sign of bone-deep filial respect. After that night, An-mei loved her mother, who wounded her own flesh in order to alleviate Popo's pain, and in order to remember what was in her bones.

## SUMMARY—LINDO JONG: "THE RED CANDLE"

*I made a promise to myself: I would always remember*
*my parents' wishes, but I would never forget myself.*
(See QUOTATIONS, *p. 70)*

Lindo Jong tells the story of her relationship with her mother. After Lindo was promised in marriage to Huang Tyan-yu at the age of two, Lindo's mother began referring to her as the daughter of Tyan-yu's mother, Huang Taitai, in order to get used to the idea that Lindo wouldn't be hers for ever. To Lindo, it felt as if Taitai, as her future mother-in-law, had already displaced Lindo's own mother. When Lindo was twelve, her house was severely damaged by a flood, and the family moved to another village. Lindo, however, went to live with Tyan-yu's family, where she was treated as a servant. She soon came to live for Taitai's praise and to think of Tyan-yu as a god.

At age sixteen, Lindo was married. On her wedding day, Lindo was filled with despair as she anticipated a life spent in pursuit of someone else's happiness. She considered drowning herself in the river, but, chancing to look out the window, she noticed the fierce wind and realized that, like the wind, she too was strong. She resolved to honor her parents' promise but to do as much for her own happiness as she could. According to custom, the matchmaker arranged for the couple to have a red candle marked with Lindo's name on one end, and Tyan-yu's on the other. The couple lit the candle, which had a wick at each end, during their marriage ceremony. A servant was instructed to watch over the candle all night, because if the candle burned until dawn without either end extinguishing prematurely, the matchmaker would declare the marriage imperishable. That night, the servant ran from the room where she was watching the candle because she mistook a thunderstorm for an attack by the Japanese. Lindo, who was walking in the courtyard, went into the room and blew out Tyan-yu's end of the candle. The next morning, however, the matchmaker displayed the candle's burnt remains and announced that the marriage was sealed. Looking at the servant, Lindo read an expression of shame and realized that the servant must have relit the candle because she feared punishment for her negligence.

For months, Tyan-yu forced Lindo to sleep on the sofa. When Taitai discovered the arrangement, Tyan-yu told his mother that Lindo was to blame. Thereafter, Lindo began sleeping in Tyan-yu's bed, but he never touched her. When Lindo failed to become pregnant, Taitai confined her to bed, saying that if Lindo remained horizontal, Tyan-yu's assumedly sowed "seed" could not become dislodged. Finally, Lindo found a way out of the marriage. She told Taitai that her ancestors came to her in a dream and said that the matchmaker's servant had allowed Tyan-yu's end of the candle to go out, which meant Tyan-yu would die if he stayed in the marriage. Lindo then convinced Taitai that the ancestors had planted the seed of Tyan-yu's child into the womb of a servant girl, secretly of imperial lineage, who was Tyan-yu's "true spiritual wife." Lindo knew that the servant girl was in fact carrying the child of a deliveryman, but the servant gratefully "confessed" to Lindo's story in order to give birth to her child in wedlock, and to marry into comfort. The marriage between Tyan-yu and Lindo was annulled, and Lindo emigrated to America.

## SUMMARY — YING-YING ST. CLAIR: "THE MOON LADY"

Ying-ying tells the story of the Moon Festival she attended when she was four. Although she can recall everything about that day, she had forgotten about it for many years. She laments that she has kept so quiet throughout her life that even her daughter Lena does not see or hear her. The reason for her reticence, Ying-ying explains, was her fear of voicing selfish desires.

On the day of the Moon Festival, Amah, Ying-ying's nurse, dressed her in a silken yellow outfit with black bands. She told Ying-ying that she would see the Moon Lady, who granted secret wishes, but cautioned that if she voiced her wishes to anyone else they would become only selfish desires. Amah told Ying-ying that it is wrong for a woman to voice her own needs, and that "[a] girl can never ask, only listen." This notion stays with Ying-ying her whole life.

The feast was held in a boat on a lake. Mesmerized, Ying-ying watched the chef kill and gut the fish for the meal. After a while, she looked down and realized that her dress was spattered with fish blood and scales. Hoping to hide the specks by dying the whole outfit red, Ying-ying smeared her clothing with some turtle blood that was being kept in the kitchen. When Amah saw her, she became angry and, after stripping off Ying-ying's bloody clothes, went to a separate part of the boat where the party was being held, leaving Ying-ying alone in her white underclothes and slippers.

Partway into the celebrations, firecrackers began to go off, and Ying-ying, startled, fell overboard into the water. A fisherman caught her in his net and pulled her into his boat. He tried to help her find her family, but when Ying-ying spotted a floating pavilion and asked the fisherman to row over to it, she found that the faces above the railings all belonged to strangers. The fisherman finally brought her ashore, where he assumed her family would find her eventually. Feeling so alone that she believed she had lost her own self, Ying-ying watched a play that was being staged about a Moon Lady, and she made a wish that she would be found.

## ANALYSIS — "SCAR," "THE RED CANDLE," & "THE MOON LADY"

An-mei's, Lindo's, and Ying-ying's stories of their childhoods in China deal with the maternal figures who influenced them and with the societal role of Chinese women in general. All three tell of how they learned of the expectation that they would sacrifice themselves for their husbands. An-mei suffered because her mother had been disowned for choosing to become a concubine rather than remaining as a widow—for refusing to sacrifice herself for her husband even after his death. Lindo lived a life of near enslavement to her future husband and mother-in-law, and then endured a marriage of further degradation, in which her bed became a kind of "prison" because she wasn't fulfilling her wifely duty of giving birth. Similarly, Ying-ying's lifelong reticence traces back to her Amah's assertion that girls should not think of their own needs, that they should "only listen" to the needs of others. On the day of the Moon Festival, Ying-ying "loses herself" not only by becoming temporarily lost from her family but by learning to stifle her own desires.

Instead of being angry with their mothers for abandoning them and for treating them coldly, An-mei, Lindo, and Ying-ying sympathize with them and attempt to excuse their mothers' actions by portraying a tradition that requires women to sacrifice their daughters. Their mothers' opinions were never asked, and they had no say in whom they married or in whether their children would be taken from them. This may account for their cold behavior: by acting sternly, they hoped to steel themselves to their pain, and to harden up their daughters, whom they knew would have to face similar sorrows. Lindo notes that her own mother, upon bidding her farewell and leaving her with the Huangs, acted with particular sternness, which Lindo knew to belie great sorrow. The Huangs were wealthier than Lindo's family, and Lindo's mother knew that marrying Tyan-yu would considerably elevate Lindo's social position and provide her with material comfort. When her mother would refer to her as Taitai's child, Lindo knew that she did not do this out of lack of love. Rather, Lindo explains, she said this only "so she wouldn't wish for something that was no longer hers." An-mei's grand mother, Popo, repeatedly said that she and her brother had fallen to earth out of the insides of a goose, like two unwanted eggs, bad-smelling and bad-tasting. But, An-mei realizes, "[s]he said this so that the ghosts would not steal us away. . . . [T]o Popo we were also very precious."

Although the characters recognize the hardships caused by a strict adherence to the patriarchal tradition, they value greatly the tradition of duty and loyalty. Their respect for custom is at odds with their sense of injustice. Thus, for example, Lindo deeply honors her mother's allegiance to the marriage contract in word and deed, whereas she scorns her daughter Waverly's American ideas about promises. To Waverly, Lindo complains that an American daughter might make a "promise" to come to dinner, but the moment that she has a headache, encounters heavy traffic, or finds that a favorite movie is showing on TV, this promise disappears. In contrast, Lindo viewed her parents' promise as her own promise, and underwent degradation and humiliation in the Huangs' home for years in order to fulfill it.

An-mei's story is also about respect for the ancient ways and the elders. She understood that her mother's attempt to cure Popo by cutting her own flesh and putting it in a soup was an act of deep love and reverence. An-mei, too, carries a scar that represents her tie to her mother. These bodily wounds function as symbols for An-mei of a daughter's corporeal bond to her mother, as reminders that one's mother is in one's bones.

Even Ying-ying remains loyal to her ancestral traditions. She felt intense pain at the way her own mother left her in the care of her Amah, and she was traumatized by the fact that no one—neither her mother nor her substitute mother, her nurse—noticed when she fell off the boat. Yet, the only person for whom Ying-ying seems to harbor any contempt is her daughter Lena. She criticizes Lena for being too Americanized, for being "lost" to her mother and her heritage, even though Ying-ying herself feels lost *because* of her heritage.

In one respect, Lindo's story diverges from An-mei's and Ying-ying's. In a manner that resembles Suyuan's willful creation of her own happiness through the Joy Luck Club, Lindo took her fate into her own hands when she saw that the price of keeping her promise to her mother, and to tradition, had become too high. Lindo explains that before her wedding, she made a second promise, a promise to herself: "I would always remember my parents' wishes, but I would never forget myself." This promise maintained and even affirmed Lindo's respect for the force of promises, but it also shows that Lindo refused to sacrifice her own identity to that force. The trick she plays on Taitai in order to extricate herself from the marriage demonstrates the power of language and imagination in directing one's own life. At the same time, however, it was an understanding of tradition that enabled Lindo to assert her own power. By playing on Taitai's cultural superstitions and reverence for her ancestors, Lindo escaped a situation of misery without suffering punishment. For, as An-mei's mother's story demonstrates, the rigidity of cultural expectation often penalizes a woman for breaking the bonds of marital sacrifice, punishing her attempt at independence with total ostracism.

## The Twenty-six Malignant Gates: Introduction, "Rules of the Game," & "The Voice from the Wall"

### Summary — Introduction

The parable that precedes the second section of the novel deals with an American-raised daughter's conflict with her mother. The mother does not want her seven-year-old daughter to ride her bicycle around the corner because her daughter will suffer an accident when she is out of sight and earshot. The mother explains that a book, titled *The Twenty-six Malignant Gates*, details the dangers that can befall her child when she is away from the protection of the home. The daughter cannot read the book because it is written in Chinese, and when her mother will not tell her what the dangers are, the girl becomes angry and rushes away on her bicycle. She falls before she reaches the corner.

### Summary — Waverly Jong: "Rules of the Game"

Lindo's daughter Waverly Jong says that when she was six, her mother taught her "the art of invisible strength," a lesson that helped her to become a child chess prodigy. She then begins the story of how her talent emerged: at Christmas, one of the members of the Jongs' church in Chinatown dressed as Santa Claus and handed out wrapped Christmas gifts, the donations of members of another church. Waverly got a multipack box of Lifesavers, and one of her brothers got a secondhand chess set that was missing two pieces. By offering two of her Lifesavers to stand in for the missing pieces, Waverly convinced her brothers, Winston and Vincent, to let her play. The winner could eat both candies. Awestruck by what she deemed to be a sort of hidden power within each piece, Waverly closely studied the dog-eared instruction booklet and borrowed chess strategy guides from the Chinatown library. She soon learned that the game hinged on invisible strength in the form of secret traps and keen foresight. After her brothers lost interest in the game, Waverly began playing with Lau Po, an old man who played chess in the park. He taught her many new strategies.

Waverly began to attract attention because of her young age, and she became a celebrity within San Francisco's Chinatown community. She played in tournaments, and by the age of nine she had become a national champion, 429 points away from grandmaster status. Lindo took great pride in her daughter's talent, and although she gave her daughter preferential treatment, she also made use of Waverly to feed her own self-pride. She would force Waverly to come to the market with her, presenting her in all the shops. One day, exasperated, Waverly yelled at her mother in the street, telling her that she was embarrassed by her constant bragging. Waverly ran off, ignoring her mother's shouts; when she returned later that night, Lindo said that because Waverly had no concern for her family, the family would have no concern for her. Waverly went into her room, lay down on the bed, and envisioned a chess game in which her mother was her opponent. Lindo's pieces were advancing across the board, pushing Waverly's pieces off; Waverly felt so dislodged that she had a feeling she would fly away; she felt she had lost her anchor. Waverly ends her story with the statement, "I closed my eyes and pondered my next move."

## SUMMARY—LENA ST. CLAIR: "THE VOICE FROM THE WALL"

Lena St. Clair says that her mother, Ying-ying, never spoke of her life in China. Lena's father, a man of English-Irish descent named Clifford, says he saved Ying-ying from a terrible tragedy that befell her in China, about which she could not bring herself to speak. Clifford knew only a few phrases in Mandarin, and Ying-ying never learned English very well. Thus, she spoke using gestures, glances, and halting English. Because he couldn't understand her, Clifford typically would put words into his wife's mouth. Although Lena understands her mother's words in Mandarin, she hardly ever understands her meanings, often considering what she says to be crazy or nonsensical. When she is forced to act as a translator for her mother, she often alters the English meanings of what others say so as to trick her mother into acting in more conventional-seeming ways; conversely, she translates her mother's odd expressions into English words that convey more mainstream thoughts.

When Clifford received a promotion, the St. Clairs moved from Oakland across the bay to an Italian neighborhood in San Francisco. The apartment, built on a steep hill, disturbed Ying-ying, who continually rearranged the furniture, claiming that things were not "balanced." Through the walls in her bedroom, Lena often heard the girl next door, Teresa Sorci, arguing with her mother. She imagined that Teresa was being killed or beaten, but whenever Lena saw her on the staircase of the building, she could never see a trace of blood or bruising on her. Soon after moving to the new apartment, Lena's parents announced to her that Ying-ying was pregnant. But although Lena's father looked forward to the baby with happiness, Ying-ying did not express joy or hope.

Ying-ying's baby, a boy, died immediately after birth from severe medical complications. Lying in her hospital bed, Ying-ying blamed herself, speaking incoherently of another son that she had killed sometime in the past. But to her father, Lena translated her mother's words into expressions of hope and consolation. After coming home, Ying-ying soon began to fall apart psychologically. Lena comforted herself by thinking that the girl next door was more miserable than she was. One day, however, Teresa knocked on the St. Clairs' door, went straight to Lena's room, and climbed onto the window ledge. She explained that her mother had locked her out and announced her intention to sneak back through her own bedroom window and shock her mother, who would be waiting for her to knock on the front door and apologize. Later that night, Lena heard Teresa and Mrs. Sorci yelling after Mrs. Sorci discovered her daughter's prank. They were screaming accusations and sobbing, but also laughing with strange joy and love.

## ANALYSIS—INTRODUCTION, "RULES OF THE GAME," & "THE VOICE FROM THE WALL"

The opening parable of "The Twenty-six Malignant Gates" presents the universal struggle between children and parents over issues of independence—the struggle over when a child should obey and admit her parent's wisdom versus when a parent should let go and allow the child to discover life for herself. The girl's mother demands adherence to certain tenets, but she refuses to give any justification for her demands, merely making vague reference to a book that her daughter cannot read because it is in Chinese. Although, to the daughter, the mother's warnings seem little more than superstition or modes of manipulation used to control her, her fall on her bicycle demonstrates the mother's almost uncanny wisdom. At the same time, however, because the mother put the idea of falling into her daughter's head, the mother's prediction may become a self-fulfilling prophecy. Whether or not the mother's warnings and restrictions signify a supernatural prescience, the daughter realizes, in her fall, that the dangers her mother fears can often be quite real. As in many of the stories in the novel, the mother's seeming tyranny or severity in fact speaks to her deep love for her daughter and her concern for her daughter's well-being.

Like the little girl in the parable, Waverly Jong attempts to defy her mother. She clashes with Lindo because she misunderstands her mother's pride in her achievements. Waverly wants chess to be strictly her own achievement, part of her own separate identity. When her mother hovers over her during her practice sessions, she feels invaded, as though her mother is somehow taking credit for what Waverly sees as her own personal strength. Moreover, Waverly is embarrassed by her mother's bragging and desire to show her off. In Waverly's next story, "Four Directions," she continues the story of her chess playing and relates that she eventually realized that her mother's pride actually functioned as an invisible support.

Although Waverly would probably be loath to admit it, her story connects thematically with her mother's ("The Red Candle"). One of the most enduring things Lindo teaches Waverly is "the art of invisible strength." Waverly uses the wind as a metaphor for this invisible strength, thus aligning herself with the same element her mother had identified with when facing her arranged marriage in China. Waverly's success with chess owes in part to her ability to gain strength through the strategically timed concealment and disclosure of secrets. This same ability was what allowed Lindo, many years before, to escape from her marriage. When Lindo learned of the servant girl's pregnancy she told no one, announcing the news at just the time she could use the revelation to her own advantage. When she lashes out at her mother, Waverly breaks her own rule. She essentially puts herself "in check" by revealing her secret weakness, her insecurities about her mother and her need to believe that her chess talent is hers alone.

While Waverly's story testifies to the strengths of hidden truths and silences, Lena's story demonstrates their dangers. Lena's mother, Ying-ying, lives in perpetual fear of unnamed dangers. She bequeaths her paranoia to her daughter by telling her stories, such as the one about Lena's great-grandfather, who had sentenced a beggar to death. According to legend, the ghost of the beggar later appeared to him, saying that in the instants preceding death he consoled himself with the thought that these final terrors would constitute the worst miseries he would ever suffer. But he was mistaken, he says: he has found that "the worst is on the other side." With these words, the ghost grabbed Lena's great-grandfather and pulled him through the wall into the land of the dead, in order to demonstrate what he meant. Both Lena and Ying-ying live in constant fear that "the worst" will invade their homes, snatch them from happiness, and pull them into agony.

Lena thus always anticipates the worst from all situations. We witness this cynicism in her story of her own wall. When Lena hears Teresa and her mother fighting through the wall of her bedroom, she imagines that someone is being killed, that a mother is taking her daughter's life. Night after night, Lena listens to the fighting and, not knowing exactly what is happening, she imagines the worst possibility. After Lena speaks with Teresa, she realizes that the Sorcis' shouting matches are their way of communicating with each other and expressing their love. Lena learns that reality does not always conform to one's most terrible fears. Although Lena has always feared what lies beyond her wall, she realizes that the worse set of circumstances may lie on the St. Clairs' side of the partition.

The tranquillity and silence of the St. Clairs' household keeps the family in a state of perpetual doubt and timidity. Lena and her father seem to fear that by probing too deeply into Ying-ying's fears and sorrows they might expose some unbearable horror. Thus, when Ying-ying lies like a statue on her bed after the baby's death, acknowledging no one, Lena's father says, "She's just tired," although both father and daughter know that the problem is much more serious. Similarly, when Lena asks her mother why she constantly rearranges the furniture, she does so only out of a feeling of duty; she in fact fears to receive a truthful answer.

By keeping silent, Ying-ying may be trying to avoid confrontation with a painful past. But by refusing to speak her feelings, she also—perhaps unwittingly—erects a kind of wall between herself and her loved ones. Thus, her family is unable to console her in the loss of the baby boy. This wall of silence, unlike the wall in the apartment, is one that no voices, no expressions of love or comfort, can penetrate.

Ying-ying does not bear sole responsibility for the emotional barrier in her home: the wall also results from problems of communication and "translation," not only of language but of culture. Lena devotes a good deal of her story to a discussion of her mother's immigration to America. Upon entering the country with his new wife, Lena's father altered Ying-ying's identity by changing her name, and also, accidentally, her birthday. She was held as a "displaced person" at the immigration station, and this image persists as a motif throughout the story. When the St. Clairs move to a new neighborhood, Lena's father sees the shift as a rise in status, but Ying-ying judges her new apartment by different standards. She deems the house out of balance and feels a sense of foreboding, but she finds herself unable to explain her fears. In part, then, her "wall" owes not to her refusal to speak out but to her actual inability to articulate (or even consciously realize) her own worries and dissatisfaction—a dissatisfaction that stems in part from her first move, from China to the United States, and from her more general failure to keep a "balance" between both sides of her life, both sides of her identity. Like the mother in the parable, Ying-ying anticipates, but cannot express, the evils that lie in store for her and her children.

## THE TWENTY-SIX MALIGNANT GATES:<br>"HALF AND HALF" & "TWO KINDS"

### SUMMARY—ROSE HSU JORDAN: "HALF AND HALF"
Rose Hsu Jordan begins by describing the Bible belonging to her mother, An-mei. Although An-mei carried the white leatherette volume with great pride for many years, the Bible now serves to prop up one of the kitchen table legs in her apartment. Rose sits at her mother's kitchen table, watches her mother sweep around the Bible, and wonders how she will break the news that she and her husband, Ted, are getting divorced. Rose knows An-mei will tell her that she

must save the marriage, but she also knows that an attempt to do so would be hopeless.

Rose remembers when she first began dating Ted. At that time, both An-mei and Mrs. Jordan, Ted's mother, had been opposed to their relationship. As a result, Rose and Ted clung to one another. Ted made all the decisions, and Rose enjoyed playing the part of Ted's maiden in distress, whom he would always save. However, after they married, Ted, a dermatologist, lost a serious malpractice suit; he lost his confidence and began forcing Rose to make some of the decisions. He became angry when she resisted, accusing her of shirking responsibility and blame. Soon afterward, Ted asked for a divorce, to Rose's utter shock.

This meditation leads into a narration of another such emotional blow, an event from Rose's childhood that scarred her and engendered An-mei's loss of religious faith. The family had taken a trip to the beach, in what Rose describes as an attempt to act like a white American family. An-mei instructed Rose to watch over her younger brothers, and because Matthew, Mark, and Luke were only a few years younger than Rose and could play together self-sufficiently, the four-year-old Bing became Rose's main responsibility. At one point during the day, Bing asked if he could walk out on the reef to where their father was fishing. Rose gave him permission, but watched him nervously as he made his way out along the crashing waves. Suddenly, Mark and Luke started a fight, and An-mei called to Rose to separate them. Rose looked up just in time to see Bing fall into the water without leaving a ripple. She stood motionless, in shock, but her sisters, returning at that moment from another stretch of the beach, instantly noticed Bing's absence. The family rushed to the water in panic. They called state authorities, but the search for Bing's body lasted hours with no success. Each person felt responsible for the accident.

Refusing to accept their fate, An-mei drove with Rose to the beach early in the morning, although to Rose's knowledge her mother had never driven before. An-mei took her Bible with her and stood on the shore, offering prayers to God. She also attempted to appease "the Coiling Dragon," whom she said had stolen Bing because one of their ancestors once stole water from a sacred well. To the Dragon, An-mei made offerings of sweetened tea and a watery-blue sapphire ring, both of which she tossed into the ocean. She also voiced to Rose her belief that her *nengkan,* her "ability to do whatever she put her mind to," would bring Bing back. Only after she threw a rescue tube into the ocean and saw it sucked away and turned to shreds did An-mei give up her search for Bing.

At the time, Rose thought that her mother had yielded to the realization that faith could not change fate. Yet Rose comments that she now realizes "fate is shaped half by expectation, half by inattention" (hence the title of the story, "Half and Half"). Just as she believes her inattention caused Bing to drown, she thinks that her inattention to signs of her marriage deteriorating resulted in Ted's request for a divorce. Rose ends her story on an optimistic note, by emphasizing the "expectation" side of fate. She concludes by returning to the Bible under the kitchen table, saying that she once flipped through it and saw her little brother's name written in the "Deaths" section, "lightly, in erasable pencil."

### Summary—Jing-mei Woo: "Two Kinds"

In the section's next story, Jing-mei speaks again. She describes her childhood, which was full of pain and resentment linked to having never become the "prodigy" that her mother desired her to be. Suyuan felt certain that Jing-mei could become a prodigy if only she tried hard enough, and at first Jing-mei eagerly complied, trying her skill at a wide range of talents. As Waverly Jong won championship after championship in chess, with Waverly's mother, Lindo, bragging day after day, Suyuan became ever more determined that she would find her daughter's hidden inner talent. But Jing-mei always fell short of her mother's expectations, and as she looked in the mirror one night, she promised herself that she would not allow her mother to try to twist her into what she was not. However, after seeing a nine-year-old Chinese girl play the piano on *The Ed Sullivan Show*, Suyuan made Jing-mei take lessons from their neighbor, a retired piano teacher named Mr. Chong. When Jing-mei discovered that Mr. Chong was deaf, and that she could get away with playing the wrong notes as long as she kept up the right rhythm, she decided to take the easy way out. As long as she kept time, she did not have to correct her mistakes.

Mr. Chong and Suyuan entered Jing-mei in a talent contest. Jing-mei played "Pleading Child" from Schumann's *Scenes from Childhood*. Everyone from the Joy Luck Club attended the show. Refusing to practice hard but still vaguely believing that her inner prodigy would emerge and allow her to play well, Jing-mei came to the recital entirely unprepared. She sat down feeling confident, but the performance proved a disaster. Two days later, when Suyuan insisted that she continue her regular schedule of practice, Jing-mei declared that she wished she were dead like her two sisters (Suyuan's long-lost children from her first marriage in China). Suyuan never mentioned piano lessons again.

Years later, Suyuan offered the family's piano to Jing-mei as a gift for her thirtieth birthday. She stated quietly that Jing-mei could have become a skilled pianist if she had tried. A few months after Suyuan's death, Jing-mei had the piano tuned. When she tried to play "Pleading Child," she was surprised how easily the music returned to her. She then played the piece on the facing page, "Perfectly Contented." After playing both pieces several times, she realized that they were complementary pieces, as if two halves of the same song.

## ANALYSIS — "HALF AND HALF" & "TWO KINDS"

Like the first two stories of the section, these latter stories examine the struggle between Chinese mothers and their Chinese American daughters. In "Half and Half," Rose Hsu recalls her mother telling her about *The Twenty-six Malignant Gates,* the book that is mentioned in the section's opening parable. She explains that every child is exposed to one particular danger on certain days, according to his or her birthday. Because the book is in Chinese, Rose is never able to understand it. Even her mother, An-mei, cannot be sure when to worry, because she cannot translate the book's dates, which use the Chinese lunar calendar, into American dates. Rose's explanation of *The Twenty-six Malignant Gates* sheds light on the section's opening parable. Did the mother in the parable know for sure that the daughter was fated to fall on her bicycle, or was she, like An-mei, constantly scared because of her inability to translate the book into English? Or was she merely anticipating the possibility that her daughter could fall? The parable makes us wonder how the fall could have been avoided: if the mother hadn't forbidden the daughter to ride around the corner, perhaps the daughter would not have become so reckless in her anger and would not have fallen at all. Yet, if the mother had said nothing, the daughter could have fallen out of sight and earshot, as the mother initially feared.

Closely connected to the section's examination of fate is its discussion of guilt and blame. After Bing's death, each member of the household feels responsible. Rose connects her reluctance to make decisions to her feelings of guilt surrounding her brother's death: not wanting to feel accountable for bad outcomes, she fears to take on any responsibility. After her husband, Ted, loses a malpractice lawsuit and is also the victim of guilt and blame, he too is unwilling to make decisions.

Rose believes that her mother also experienced feelings of guilt and resignation. She asserts that her mother lost her faith in God after Bing's death. As evidence, she points to the way An-mei stopped carrying her Bible to church and began using it as a wedge under a too-short leg of the kitchen table. Because Rose herself sank into passivity after Bing's death, she assumes her mother reacted the same way. Yet, by the end of her story, she also notices that her mother sweeps the Bible off and keeps it from gathering dust. The fact that Bing's name is written under the heading "Deaths" in erasable pencil demonstrates that An-mei still values the Bible enough to find meaning in the act of inscribing her dead son's name there. The erasable pencil speaks to her belief that Bing might still live. After the loss of Bing, An-mei may have become less openly religious, but she never resigned herself to thinking that human beings have no control over what happens to them. Thus, when Rose asks why she should try to save her marriage, saying there is no hope, no reason to try, An-mei responds that she should try simply "because [she] must. . . . This is not hope. Not reason. This is your fate . . . what you must do." Rose believes her mother is bitter and hardened from Bing's death, but her story about her marriage shows that Rose herself suffered the most lasting emotional damage.

Jing-mei's story also deals with a clash between a mother's faith and belief in persistence versus a daughter's inner sense of futility. Jing-mei believes that she is simply not "fated" to be a prodigy, that ultimately there resides within her an unchangeable element of mediocrity. When she tells her reflection in the mirror one night that she will not allow her mother to change her, that she will not try to be what she is not, she asserts her will in a strong but negative manner. At that moment, she recalls, she saw the "prodigy side" of herself in the anger and determination that were in her face. This comment suggests that "prodigy" is really one's will, one's desire to succeed. In retrospect, Jing-mei muses that perhaps she never gave herself a chance at the piano because she never devoted her will to trying.

Neither Jing-mei nor Suyuan is completely to blame for the piano recital disaster. It is Suyuan's incessant nagging and insinuations regarding her daughter's inadequacies that partially drive Jing-mei to refuse to practice seriously. The pain Jing-mei feels after the recital stems not just from her own failure but also from her shame in having disappointed her mother. This shame will persist into her adult life, as she continues to fall short of her mother's expectations. Perhaps Jing-mei's shame in fact stems from her guilt in having willed her own failure.

Suyuan's inflated expectations and excessive pressure backfire, contributing to Jing-mei's failure to achieve what she might have achieved if left to herself. Yet, at the same time, the disastrous piano recital also testifies to the power of Suyuan's love for Jing-mei, and to her faith in her daughter's ability. The immense energy that Suyuan devotes to the search for Jing-mei's "inner prodigy"—cleaning for her piano teacher, saving up for a used piano—demonstrates that her motivations probably lie deeper than the promise of bragging rights at church each Sunday. Many years later, Jing-mei realizes that Suyuan's attempt to bring out her "prodigy" expressed her deep faith in her daughter's abilities rather than her desire to make her something she was not.

At the end of her narrative, Jing-mei adds that Suyuan offered her the piano for her thirtieth birthday, a gesture that shows that Suyuan understands the reasons behind Jing-mei's refusal to play: Jing-mei did not regard the piano lessons as something she did for herself. By offering the piano to her daughter as a gift, Suyuan gives Jing-mei the opportunity to try again without feeling as though she is doing so for someone else's benefit. Although Jing-mei says she did not take the piano right away, she is comforted by Suyuan's expression of faith in her ability to do what she wanted.

Sadly, Jing-mei did not understand until after Suyuan's death that her conflicts with her mother did not arise from any cruel expectations on Suyuan's part but from Suyuan's love and faith in her— even when Jing-mei failed, or even purposefully failed, to live up to that faith. Jing-mei comes to this understanding when she sits at the recently tuned piano, Suyuan's peace offering, and tries to play Schumann's "Pleading Child" once again. When she plays the piece on the facing page, "Perfectly Contented," and realizes that the two are "two halves of the same song," Jing-mei is articulating the fact that she has journeyed psychologically from a place of pained longing for her mother's acceptance to a place of understanding why her mother pushed her so hard: the pleading child has come to a place of contentment, though the path she has taken may be littered with regrets.

# AMERICAN TRANSLATION: INTRODUCTION, "RICE HUSBAND," & "FOUR DIRECTIONS"

## SUMMARY—INTRODUCTION

In the parable that precedes the third section, a mother visits her daughter's new condominium. She expresses dismay at the mirror her daughter has placed at the foot of the bed: she believes superstitiously that this mirror will cause her daughter's marriage happiness to bounce back and deflect away. Her daughter dismisses the warning as just another example of her mother's tendency to see everything as inauspicious. The mother then pulls out a second mirror, which she had bought as a housewarming gift, and places it at the head of the bed: the mirrors reflecting each other will multiply the daughter's "peach-blossom luck," she says. When the daughter asks her mother to explain this luck, the mother points into the mirror, and says that she can see her future grandchild. The daughter looks and sees the child in her own reflection.

## SUMMARY—LENA ST. CLAIR: "RICE HUSBAND"

Lena St. Clair, who discussed her childhood in "The Voice from the Wall," begins by explaining how her mother has always been able to predict the evils that will affect their family. Now, says Lena, Ying-ying regrets never having done anything to prevent them. Lena wonders what her mother's insights will reveal when she visits Lena and her husband, Harold, in their new home.

Lena thinks back to another instance of her mother's predictive powers. Her mother had told her once that her future husband would have one pock mark on his face for every grain of rice Lena did not finish at dinner, and Lena had thought of a neighbor boy named Arnold, who had a pitted face. The boy had always treated Lena like a bully, and thus, to avoid having to marry him, the young Lena scraped every last grain of rice from her bowl: now she would marry only a smooth-faced man. Yet Ying-ying reminded Lena that for many years she had habitually left grains standing in her bowl. Terrified that she was fated to marry Arnold, Lena began to loathe her neighbor and wish for his death.

In Lena's mind, the connection between her eating and its effect on whether or not she would marry Arnold soon progressed to a causal connection between her eating and the well-being of Arnold himself. The rice conceptually evoked his rice-grain-sized pock marks, and she believed that by leaving her rice, she would cause him to develop more marks. She refused to finish large portions of every kind of food, believing that they would somehow transfer into maladies on Arnold's body. Five years later, although she had long forgotten Arnold, she had become addicted to not eating and was suffering from anorexia. When she learned that the seventeen-year-old Arnold had suddenly died of an extremely rare measles-related illness, she gorged herself on ice cream and spent the night throwing it up. Looking back, Lena knows that she cannot logically blame herself for Arnold's death, and yet she wonders whether she might have willed it, whether Arnold was in fact "destined" to be her husband. Even when she dismisses these thoughts, she questions whether her evil intentions caused her to end up with her present husband as a punishment for wanting to kill her "destined" husband.

Ever since Lena and Harold met, they have kept strict accounts of the money each has spent, even when dining out together, and have shared very little other than expenses. Harold took Lena's advice and started his own architecture firm, but because he was so intent on keeping their accounts separate, he refused her offer of a loan. Instead, he asked her to move in with him—she would pay half of his apartment rent, which meant he would be able to put that money toward his firm. Within a year, Lena was working for Harold as a project coordinator, and she essentially developed his entire business concept by suggesting that he specialize in "thematic restaurant" design. Despite the fact that she works hard and shows great talent, Harold refuses to promote Lena because he does not want to appear to be unfairly favoring his wife. He now earns seven times more than she does. Lena becomes upset when she thinks about what it means to be Harold's domestic "equal."

When Ying-ying visits, she notices the list of all the prices of shared items that Lena and Harold have bought for the house. When Lena explains the list, Ying-ying states that Lena should not be expected to pay back Harold for buying ice cream, because Lena has hated ice cream ever since her terrible vomiting incident. Later that night, Lena decides to mention her hatred of ice cream to Harold, who claims that he always supposed Lena abstained from it merely as part of her frequent diets. Although Harold willingly agrees to pay for the ice cream himself, Lena's feelings of aggression toward him are not alleviated. Unsure of the source of her anger, she picks a fight. Suddenly, Ying-ying breaks a vase on Harold's wobbly table in the guest room. Harold had designed and built the table himself during his student days, and when Ying-ying saw it in the guest room, she asked why Lena used it. "You put something else on top, everything fall down," she says. Lena cleans up the glass and tells Ying-ying not to worry; she knew this would happen eventually. Ying-ying asks why Lena hasn't done anything to prevent it.

### SUMMARY—WAVERLY JONG: "FOUR DIRECTIONS"

Waverly Jong wants to tell her mother, Lindo, that she is engaged to her live-in boyfriend, Rich, so she takes Lindo to Four Directions, a Chinese restaurant Waverly likes. Every time Waverly mentions Rich, however, Lindo changes the subject. Waverly invites Lindo to her apartment to show her the mink coat Rich gave her. Her apartment is littered with Rich's belongings, so Waverly knows that Lindo cannot ignore the seriousness of their relationship. But Lindo says nothing about the evidence of Rich's presence in the apartment.

Waverly returns to the story that she began in "Rules of the Game"—the story of her childhood chess talent and her disagreement with Lindo over Lindo's constant bragging in public. After days of silence between her and her mother, Waverly decided to quit chess temporarily. She initiated the break by purposefully missing a tournament. Although Waverly had meant to hurt Lindo by skipping the event, Lindo was not upset; Waverly alone suffered, as she knew that she could have easily beaten the boy who won. Soon, Waverly broke the silence to tell Lindo that she had decided to play again. Although she expected her mother to react joyously, Lindo was reproachful and told Waverly that it is not so easy to quit and begin again so glibly.

Lindo no longer polished Waverly's trophies, and she stopped hovering over her as she practiced. Waverly lost her next tournament, and other defeats followed. Her once steady confidence vanished, and she felt as though the wind had gone out of her sails. At age fourteen, Waverly gave up chess entirely.

Waverly describes her first husband, Marvin. Lindo used to criticize him, and Waverly feels that this criticism poisoned her marriage, as it caused her to see only Marvin's faults. Now she fears that Lindo will spoil her marriage to Rich as well. She knows that if the marriage failed it would crush Rich, for he loves her unconditionally, the way she loves her own little daughter, the child she had with Marvin, Shoshana.

Waverly brings Rich to dinner at her mother's house, intending to break the news at last. However, Rich unwittingly commits several blunders in etiquette during dinner, so Waverly does not mention their marriage plans. The next day, Waverly visits her mother, ready to unload her burden of anger and resentment, but when she arrives she finds Lindo asleep. Seeing her mother looking so innocent and powerless, Waverly breaks down and begins to cry. When she wakes, Lindo reveals that she has known all along about the engagement, and she expresses surprise at Waverly's assumption that she hates Rich. Waverly realizes that she has long misunderstood her mother. She adds that she and Rich have postponed their wedding because Lindo told them they should wait until October to take their honeymoon in China. Waverly contemplates inviting Lindo to come with them. Even though she knows a joint trip would prove a disaster, she believes the trip could help the women to reconcile their differences.

## ANALYSIS—INTRODUCTION, "RICE HUSBAND," & "FOUR DIRECTIONS"

The parable that opens this section of the book highlights the irrational nature of superstitious beliefs, but also emphasizes the deep wisdom that often lies hidden inside them. The mother's seemingly ridiculous paranoia about the positioning of the mirror annoys her daughter, who wants to decorate her new home according to her own wishes, to make her own decisions based on her own reasoning.

The daughter probably sees her mother's gift of a second mirror as another infringement upon her ability to assert her own preferences and taste. Yet, when the mother claims that her future grandchild is visible in the mirror, the text affirms the mother's words, with the phrase, "There it was." There may indeed be some truth to the grandchild's presence in the mirror, because the grandchild will, in many ways, be a reflection of the daughter, just as the daughter reflects many of her own mother's qualities. It seems that perhaps the daughter, who is impatient with her mother's superstitious beliefs, has underestimated her mother's insight. In any case, what does shine clearly from the mirror is the mother's deep love for her daughter.

The stories in "American Translation" explore superstition: its irrationality, the annoyance and even harm that it can cause, its occasional intersections with deep wisdom. The stories also examine notions of other cultural barriers between mother and daughter—often in the form of taste—and the ways in which, despite the barriers that seem to differentiate them so markedly, daughters nevertheless resemble and reflect their mothers.

Ying-ying's unexplained, superstitious fears and constant anticipation of tragedy have contributed to a similar, "reflected" attitude of fatalism in Lena. When Lena was young, her mother's warnings about her failure to finish all her rice engendered a sense that she lacked all control over her life and whom she would marry. This in turn led to Lena's attempts to gain control. At first, she manipulated her eating so as to "kill" Arnold and avoid marrying him; later, even after she had forgotten all about Arnold, she tried to maintain control by restricting her eating more strictly, to the point of anorexia. Yet she remains convinced that she lives in a world of forces that exceed human control: this causes her to passively accept the imbalance and lack of fulfillment in her marriage as her fate, rather than trying to speak up for herself.

Lena is blind to the factors that contributed to her fatalism. Clifford used to speak for Ying-ying, and Lena similarly allows Harold to define what "equality" in their marriage means. In effect, he is a partner in the marriage, but she is an associate—just as she is in the architecture firm. Harold states their marriage is stronger because it is based on equality rather than money. However, because his idea of equality is based on money, the marriage is as well.

Ying-ying uses Harold's wobbly table, a project from his days as an architecture student, to show Lena that her marriage is wildly out of balance. She wants Lena to *do* something about the imbalance rather than silently accept it as fate. After years of suffering, Ying-ying finally knows that expressing one's wishes is not selfish, as her Amah had told her. She does not want her daughter to make the same mistake of remaining passively silent. The interchange over the toppled table exudes double meaning: Lena says she knew it would happen, and Ying-ying asks her why she did nothing to prevent it. The "it" here refers not only to the shattering of the vase but to the shattering of Lena's marriage.

Waverly's story examines a mother's place in her daughter's life. As Waverly comes to see her mother as an invincible opponent in life, she focuses too much on her metaphoric chess match against Lindo, neglecting her actual chess matches. She intends to attack Lindo by sacrificing chess, but her move only hurts herself, and Waverly believes that Lindo has planned it this way. In the heat of battle, Waverly loses sight of her original goal of persuading Lindo to allow her space and independence. When Waverly declares her intention to return to chess, she thinks that with this simple move she can placate her mother and heal all wounds. But, as Lindo tells Waverly, "it is not so easy." While she is referring to Waverly's capricious and ungrateful treatment of her talent for chess, Lindo also means that the mother-daughter relationship is not so easily patched—that Waverly cannot expect to turn her mother into a pawn.

When Waverly returns to chess to find her prodigy gone, she realizes that part of what sustained her had been her mother's love and support. Although she believed that the talent was all her own and that her mother was taking undue credit for her successes, she now sees that her achievements always depended in part upon her mother's devotion and pride in her. Now a mother herself, Waverly has come to understand the nature of a mother's inviolable love. She sees that this is what Lindo was expressing all those years, even in her criticism and nagging. Here again the motifs of the parable reemerge. Waverly sees herself in her mother as she develops her relationship to her own daughter; she recognizes more fully the power of maternal love.

The cultural tensions seen in the opening parable also shine through in Waverly's story. Waverly anticipates that Lindo will dislike her white boyfriend, Rich, but Waverly cringes as much as anyone else at Rich's culturally ignorant series of faux pas at dinner. She comes to realize that for years she projected her own anxieties through her mother, turning her into a spiteful, critical, and uncompromising woman. When she finally speaks to her mother openly about Rich, she realizes that Lindo's criticism only expresses her deep concern for Waverly's well-being, her profound desire for her daughter to know the happiness of marriage that she was deprived of for so many years in China.

## American Translation: "Without Wood" & "Best Quality"

### Summary—Rose Hsu Jordan: "Without Wood"

> *"A mother is best. A mother knows what is inside you,"*
> *she said. . . . "A psyche-atricks will only make you*
> *hulihudu, make you see heimongmong."*
> *(See* Quotations, *p. 71)*

Rose Hsu Jordan describes finding divorce papers and a ten-thousand-dollar check from her husband, Ted, in her mailbox. Paralyzed with shock and pain, she leaves them in a drawer for two weeks while she tries to decide what to do. She stays in bed for three days, mostly unconscious, with the help of sleeping pills. Finally, she is wakened by a phone call from An-mei, who asks her why she refuses to speak up for herself. Ted calls a few minutes later to ask why she has not yet signed and returned the divorce papers. He announces that he wants the house because he now plans to marry someone else. After the initial shock, Rose laughs and tells him to come to the house to pick up his papers. When he arrives, Rose gives him the papers still unsigned and announces that she will not be leaving the house. She refuses to allow him to uproot her and throw her away.

## SUMMARY — JING-MEI WOO: "BEST QUALITY"

A few months before her death, Suyuan cooked a crab dinner for ten people to celebrate the Chinese New Year. As she and Jing-mei shopped together in Chinatown for the ingredients, Suyuan explained that the feistiest crabs are of the best quality; even beggars would reject a crab that has died before being cooked. During the marketing, Suyuan grumbled about the tenants who lived above her in the building she owned. When the couple's cat disappeared, they accused Suyuan of having poisoned it. Jing-mei wondered whether her mother did poison the cat, but she knew not to question her.

While the two women were choosing crabs, the leg of one of the crabs became detached, and the grocer demanded that Suyuan pay for the creature. Suyuan thus bought eleven instead of ten, stating that the damaged crab would be extra. Back at home, Jing-mei could not bear to watch crabs being cooked, though she knew in her rational mind that the crabs probably lacked brains big enough to realize what was happening to them.

The Jongs and their children attended the dinner. Vincent brought his girlfriend, Lisa, and Waverly brought Rich and Shoshana. Mr. Chong, Jing-mei's old piano teacher, was also invited. Suyuan had not counted Shoshana when buying the crabs, but Waverly now carefully chose the best crab and gave it to her daughter before choosing the next best two for herself and Rich. The rest of the party continued to pick the best crabs until there were two left, one of which was the crab missing a leg. Jing-mei tried to take the defective crab, but Suyuan insisted she take the better one. Suyuan then sniffed her crab, and took it into the kitchen to throw away, veiling the trip by returning with more seasonings for the table.

Waverly complimented Jing-mei's haircut and was shocked to learn that Jing-mei still went to her gay stylist. Waverly warned Jing-mei that the stylist might have AIDS and urged her to consider using her own stylist, Mr. Rory, instead. Waverly added that Mr. Rory's prices might be too high, deliberately referring to Jing-mei's less successful career. Infuriated, Jing-mei mentioned that Waverly's law firm had not paid her for some freelance work she had done, writing a publicity brochure, and after several insults from Jing-mei, Waverly replied that her firm had decided not to use Jing-mei's work, adding that she had only praised the work to Jing-mei because she didn't want to hurt her feelings. Jing-mei offered to revise the brochure, but Waverly refused, mocking the quality of the work she submitted. Jing-mei cleared the table and retreated to the kitchen, fighting back tears.

After the guests left, Suyuan joined her daughter in the kitchen. Suyuan explained that she did not eat the legless crab because it had died before she cooked it. She teased Jing-mei for choosing the worse of the two remaining crabs, because anyone else would have taken the better one—the "best quality" available. She remarked that Jing-mei's way of thinking differed from that of most people. She gave Jing-mei a jade pendant, telling her that it was her "life's importance." She advised Jing-mei not to listen to Waverly, whose words always "move sideways" like a crab, and explained that Jing-mei could and should move in a different direction. Now, at the time of Jing-mei's reminiscence, she is cooking dinner for her father. The upstairs tenants' tomcat jumps onto the windowsill outside, and Jing-mei is relieved to see that her mother didn't kill it—the cat is alive and well.

### ANALYSIS—"WITHOUT WOOD" & "BEST QUALITY"

As throughout *The Joy Luck Club,* in these sections we see that a mother's seemingly paranoid intuitions, groundless hunches, and unwelcome meddling are frequently on target and represent a loving rather than critical mind-set. When Rose first tells An-mei that Ted has sent her a check for ten thousand dollars, An-mei asks if that means he is having an affair; Rose laughs in response to her suggestion. However, she later notices that the garden in her home has gone untended for quite some time: this had been Ted's task, and he had once shown almost obsessive care for it. Once, Rose's fortune cookie stated that if a man neglected his garden, he was thinking about pulling up roots. When she talks to Ted on the phone, he tells her that he wants the divorce to move quickly because he wants to remarry and move back into the house—An-mei's instincts were on target all along. She also seems correct now in urging Rose to take action and not remain passive.

By refusing to sign the divorce papers quickly, Rose allows herself the time to ponder what she wants and what her marriage means to her. She learns that Ted has been planning to uproot her from his life all along. Once she has the necessary information, Rose decides that she won't allow Ted to bully her into doing what will best suit him. Her mother has often told her that she lacks "wood"—the element that gives people what we would call a strong backbone, the ability to refuse to give way in the face of hardships or aggression from others. Now, Rose realizes that her mother was right. Yet although Rose now recognizes her excessive indecisiveness, she also sees that Ted's frequent harangues against her inability to make decisions allowed him to tacitly and unfairly blame her for all the problems in their marriage.

Jing-mei's story also deals with superstition blending into wisdom. Again, cultural tensions emerge as a motif. At the beginning of her narrative, Jing-mei describes her first reaction to the "life's importance" pendant; she had found it garish and unstylish, yet since her mother's death she has come to realize its meaning. Once symbolizing only a cultural difference between herself and her mother, the pendant has now become a testament to the maternal wisdom and love that Jing-mei once mistook—indeed, perhaps due to cultural differences—for superstition and criticism.

Suyuan asserts that a crab that has died before it is cooked will taste bad and that a missing leg on a crab is a bad sign on the Chinese New Year. Jing-mei seems to find these beliefs silly; yet, at the same time, she exhibits the same admittedly irrational thoughts when she sympathizes with the boiling crabs. Moreover, Suyuan's seemingly illogical conceptual linkages between the crabs and the women's lives later prove rather insightful: while she seems to display a certain foolishness in drawing causal connections between the crabs' fate and human fate, she proves her insight when she later draws a metaphorical connection between a crab's movement and the way Waverly conducts her life, always looking sideways out of the corner of her eye at potential competitors, making jabs at people while veiling them as innocent comments.

When Suyuan gives Jing-mei the jade pendant, Jing-mei thinks that the gift is meant merely as a sign of sympathy after her humiliating interchange with Waverly. But Suyuan explains the meaning of the gift: she has worn the pendant against her skin; now Jing-mei can wear it, too, and absorb from it Suyuan's love. Suyuan presents the pendant to Jing-mei at this moment not out of pity but out of pride: she has ceased to measure Jing-mei against Waverly, having recognized the fundamental differences in their personalities and their motivations. Jing-mei's behavior during dinner shed light on these differences: while everyone else at the table chooses his or her crab in a spirit of selfishness and competition, Jing-mei chooses the worse of the two remaining crabs because she wants her mother to enjoy the better one. Suyuan recognizes the flip side to what she had always seen as Jing-mei's lack of ambition—her humility and modesty, which can often translate into generosity and selflessness. At times, this is the "best quality" one can have. Suyuan acknowledges and celebrates this aspect of her daughter with the gift of the pendant.

## QUEEN MOTHER OF THE WESTERN SKIES: INTRODUCTION, "MAGPIES," & "WAITING BETWEEN THE TREES"

### SUMMARY—INTRODUCTION
The opening parable of the fourth section depicts the woman of the first three parables as she plays with a baby granddaughter. She laments that she does not know whether to teach her granddaughter to shed her innocence in order to protect herself from emotional injury or to preserve her granddaughter's optimism and faith in human goodness. The woman regrets having taught her daughter (the baby's mother) to recognize the evil in people, because she suspects that to recognize evil in others is to yield to the evil in oneself. The baby begins to laugh, and the woman takes her laugh as a sign of wisdom. The baby, the woman says, is really the "Queen Mother of the Western Skies," who has lived many times and has come back to answer the woman's questions about evil. The woman tells her granddaughter that she has learned her lesson: one must lose one's innocence but not one's hope; one must never stop laughing. The woman tells the baby to teach her mother the same lesson.

### SUMMARY—AN-MEI HSU: "MAGPIES"
In this final section of the novel, the mothers again resume their narratives. An-mei Hsu tells the first story. She begins by brooding on

her daughter Rose's decaying marriage. She remarks that although Rose believes she has run out of choices, Rose is in fact making a distinct choice in refusing to speak up for herself. An-mei knows this, she says, because she was taught to desire nothing, to absorb other people's misery, to suppress her own pain. She received her first lesson in such passive stoicism when she was a young girl living at her uncle's house in Ningpo. An-mei's mother came and cut her own flesh for her mother, Popo, who was dying (see the story "Scar").

After Popo's death, An-mei's mother prepared to leave, and An-mei began to cry. Her mother told her that once, when she was a girl, she had sat crying by the pond when a turtle surfaced, swallowing her teardrops as they touched the water. The turtle then said that he had eaten her tears and therefore knew her misery. He warned her that if she continued to cry, her life would always be sad. He spat out the tears in the form of tiny eggs, which cracked open to reveal seven fluttering magpies, birds of joy. The turtle said that whenever one cries, one is not washing away one's sorrows but feeding another's joy. For this reason, one must learn to swallow one's own tears.

An-mei's mother wanted to take An-mei with her. An-mei's uncle told her she would ruin her daughter's life as she had ruined her own. An-mei, defying the angry exhortations of her aunt and uncle, decided to leave with her mother. They allowed her to go, but her uncle deemed her "finished." An-mei's one deep regret was that her brother could not come along. Mother and daughter traveled to Tientsin, where An-mei's mother had lived for the past five years in the household of a rich merchant named Wu Tsing. She lived with him as his third concubine, or "fourth wife." The house was a huge Western-style mansion, full of luxuries and amusements, including a European cuckoo clock. An-mei lived in glorious happiness for a few weeks, until Wu Tsing returned home from his travels accompanied by a young and beautiful fifth wife, who replaced An-mei's mother as the latest concubine. An-mei's mother became depressed at her sudden decline in status and dignity.

Soon the winter came, and Wu Tsing's second and third wives returned to Tientsin from their summer homes. Second Wife, an expensively dressed, older woman of forty-five, appeared especially intimidating to An-mei. Although she seemed a bit too old to still have young children, she carried in her arms a two-year-old son, Syaudi. Upon first meeting An-mei, Second Wife gave her a pearl necklace. An-mei felt honored by the attention, but her mother warned her not to be manipulated by Second Wife. Later, An-mei's mother crushed one "pearl" of the necklace under her shoe, proving to An-mei that it was made of mere glass. Afterward, An-mei's mother gave her a sapphire ring.

Yan Chang, the servant of An-mei's mother, explained to An-mei that Wu Tsing's original wife, known as First Wife, bore children with physical deformities or large birthmarks, thus failing to produce a suitable heir. She took many pilgrimages to honor Buddha, hoping to rectify her misfortune with a perfect child. Yet she had no more children. Wu Tsing gave her money for her own household. Twice a year, she visited his house, but she remained in her bedroom smoking opium. One day An-mei's mother informed her that Wu Tsing had arranged for them soon to have their own household as well.

Yan Chang also told An-mei the story behind Second Wife. She had been a famous singer, and Wu Tsing had married her for the prestige of having a wife everyone else desired. Second Wife soon discovered how to control Wu Tsing's money: knowing his fear of ghosts, she would stage fake suicides by eating raw opium, thus making herself sick. Wu Tsing, afraid that she would come back as a ghost and reap revenge on him, would raise her allowance each time in an attempt to make her spirit less vengeful in case she should indeed die. Yet there was one thing Second Wife could not control: she could not have children, and she knew that Wu Tsing wanted an heir. She thus found a woman to become his third wife, but she made sure that the woman was quite ugly and would thus not replace Second Wife in Wu Tsing's heart. Later, when Third Wife bore only daughters, Second Wife arranged for Wu Tsing to marry An-mei's mother.

Yan Chang claims that An-mei's mother is too good for the family. Five years earlier, she had been tricked into marriage with Wu Tsing when she and Yan Chang were visiting a Buddhist pagoda to "kowtow," or worship. The pagoda was on a lake, and on the way back, Yan Chang and An-mei's mother shared a boat with Wu Tsing and Second Wife. Second Wife had been searching for a third concubine for Wu Tsing who would keep him from wasting his money in the teahouses and give him a son. She could tell that An-mei's mother was in mourning (her husband, a Buddhist scholar, had died one year earlier) from her white clothes, but she devised a scheme. She invited her for dinner and an evening of mahjong. After it became too late for An-mei's mother to travel home, Second Wife had her sleep in her bed with her. In the middle of the night, Second Wife and Wu Tsing switched places, and Wu Tsing raped An-mei's mother. Second Wife then announced to everyone that An-mei's mother had seduced Wu Tsing. Entirely disgraced, An-mei's mother had no choice but to marry Wu Tsing. She gave birth to a son, Syaudi, whom Second Wife took as her own. A few days after Yan Chang revealed this story to An-mei, Second Wife staged another fake suicide and prevented An-mei and her mother from getting the second household they had been promised.

Two days before the lunar new year, An-mei's mother committed suicide. Although Yan Chang suspected that hers was a fake suicide gone wrong, An-mei realized that the act was quite deliberate. Before dying, her mother told An-mei that she was killing her weak spirit to make An-mei's spirit stronger. Chinese folklore states that the soul returns on the third day after death to "settle scores." Wu Tsing, wanting to avoid a vengeful spirit, promised her spirit that he would raise An-mei and Syaudi as his "honored children" in addition to honoring her as he would a First Wife. Afterward, An-mei confronted Second Wife with the fake pearl necklace, crushing it underfoot. She says it was on that day that she learned to shout.

## SUMMARY—YING-YING ST. CLAIR: "WAITING BETWEEN THE TREES"

> [W]hen [my daughter] was born, she sprang from me like a slippery fish, and has been swimming away ever since. All her life, I have watched her as though from another shore.
>
> *(See* QUOTATIONS, *p. 72)*

Ying-ying St. Clair notes her daughter Lena's marital situation with great sadness. She says that she has always known a thing before it happens, and that the signs of her daughter's broken marriage are clear to her, although Lena cannot see them.

Ying-ying remembers her first marriage, about which she has never told Lena. She was raised in a very wealthy household. When she was sixteen, a vulgar older man who was a friend of the family began to show interest in her. Although he repulsed Ying-ying, she instantly felt that she was destined to marry him. The marriage was arranged, and Ying-ying soon came to love the man, as if against her own will. She tried to please him in every way, and she conceived a child that she knew, in her almost telepathic manner, would be a son. Several months into the pregnancy, her husband left her for an opera singer, and Ying-ying learned that he had committed infidelities throughout their marriage. In her rage and sorrow, she aborted her unborn son.

Ying-ying explains that she was born in the year of the Tiger. The Tiger spirit has two natures: the golden nature is fierce, and the black nature is cunning and crafty, waiting between the trees. Ying-ying explains that only after her husband left her did she learn to use the black side of her spirit. She lived for ten years with relatives before she decided to get a job in a clothing shop, where, one day, she met an American merchant named Clifford St. Clair. "Saint," as Ying-ying calls him, courted Ying-ying for four years, but she waited for news of her renegade husband's death before marrying Clifford. Clifford believed she was a poor village girl and had no idea that Ying-ying had grown up amidst an opulence greater than any he could provide. She did not tell him of her former life until many years after they were married. The first marriage had already drained her spirit to such an extent that as soon as she stopped having to struggle to live, she became the ghost of the tiger she had once been. Ying-ying has decided to make a change, because she is ashamed that Lena, her daughter who was also born under the sign of the Tiger, also lacks the spirit that should be hers by right of her birth year. She resolves to share her painful, secret past with Lena in order to cut her Tiger spirit loose.

ANALYSIS

The parable that introduces the last section of *The Joy Luck Club* centers on the cyclical nature of inheritance. As the grandmother broods, she hears a wisdom in the baby's laughter and decides that the baby is Syi Wang Mu, Queen Mother of the Western Skies, already reborn infinite times, come to counsel her grandmother and mother. Thus, the grandmother notes that wisdom can be passed both ways—from old to young, but also young to old. Each generation can offer valuable lessons to the others.

The woman in the parable also realizes that many lessons will not come naturally and must be taught to her granddaughter. In the stories that follow the parable, the three mothers recognize their own flaws and virtues manifested in their daughters, and they worry about how to keep their daughters from suffering the same pains they suffered. An-mei's mother teaches her two different lessons. The first, which she teaches through the story of the turtle, is to swallow her tears and suppress her bitterness. The second, which she teaches by crushing a pearl from Second Wife's necklace, is to see beyond appearances. This second lesson proves useful to An-mei, as it teaches her to be on guard against deceit. An-mei in turn passes this lesson on to her daughter Rose, so that Rose sees through Ted's manipulative ways: she realizes that he wants to get out of his marriage with the house and most of the money, so he can quickly move a new wife into Rose's place.

However, An-mei's mother's first lesson—that one should swallow one's own tears—proves harmful, first to An-mei's mother herself, then to An-mei, and then to Rose, to whom An-mei passes it on unwittingly. An-mei reflects on this phenomenon, saying that even though she tried to teach her daughter to speak up for herself, Rose followed in her mother's footsteps. An-mei remarks that only after her own mother's suicide did she learn "to shout"—to assert herself—when she confronted Second Wife. An-mei recognizes that while passivity and reticence may once have been the only option for women, women no longer need live this way. She wonders now how to rectify the seemingly irrepressible force of inheritance, how to extricate her mother's passivity from her daughter. The text implies that the answer may lie in the power of storytelling.

An-mei's mother sacrifices herself for the sake of her child. When she sees that her declining status in Wu Tsing's household would mean a lower status for An-mei as an adult, she commits suicide, forcing Wu Tsing to promise to give An-mei a respected rank in his household and removing her from Second Wife's clutches. An-mei comes to manifest the same maternal devotion later in her life. In "Half and Half," Rose tells the story of An-mei's incessant search for her son Bing. An-mei throws the sapphire ring her mother gave her into the ocean to appease the evil spirits keeping Bing's body, even though the ring, which we learn in this story was given to An-mei when she was a child, seems to have been An-mei's only memento of her mother. Yet, An-mei's sacrifice of the ring commemorates her mother's own act of devotion by repeating it in a new form.

Like An-mei, Ying-ying worries that she has unintentionally handed down her passivity to her daughter Lena. As their earlier stories have demonstrated, for Ying-ying and Lena, passivity interweaves itself with fatalism and prevents them from taking initiative. In "Waiting Between the Trees" Ying-ying believed that she was "destined" to marry her husband, despite her dislike of him, so she made no real effort to resist, and the tragic course of events that followed destroyed her spirit. After she aborted her child, Ying-ying thought she would take advantage of the cunning, "black," side of her Tiger spirit and wait for a ripe opportunity to reenter life in full force. However, when she meets Clifford St. Clair, Ying-ying displays the same fatalism that led her to her first marriage disaster. Although she neither likes nor dislikes the foreign merchant, she "knows" that he embodies a message: that the black side of her would soon fade away. Later, in America, Ying-ying passively watches Lena grow up as if they stand on separate shores. Nonetheless, she has realized that her inaction has been a bad example for her daughter. She resolves to share the story of her past mistakes with Lena so that Lena's own Tiger spirit will waken to action.

An-mei and Ying-ying both suffer traumatic experiences that destroy their innocence. An-mei recovers from her grief, taking with her important knowledge about trust and faith, but Ying-ying has only begun to recover from her painful first marriage. She is roused to confront her past because Lena's marriage is in trouble—Ying-ying's story demonstrates, like the parable that precedes it, that the older generation can and does learn from the younger one.

## QUEEN MOTHER OF THE WESTERN SKIES: "DOUBLE FACE" & "A PAIR OF TICKETS"

### SUMMARY—LINDO JONG: "DOUBLE FACE"

*How can she think she can blend in? Only her skin and her hair are Chinese. Inside—she is all American-made.*
*(See QUOTATIONS, p. 73)*

Lindo Jong discusses her daughter Waverly, who is planning her wedding and honeymoon to China with Rich. To Lindo, Waverly has expressed her fear that she will blend in so well with the Chinese that she won't be allowed to return to America. When Lindo replies that the Chinese will know Waverly is American before she even opens her mouth, Waverly is disappointed. Lindo reproaches herself for having tried to make her daughter half Chinese and half American, when such a combination is impossible. She regrets not having taught Waverly enough about her Chinese heritage.

Before her wedding, Waverly takes Lindo to her fashionable hair stylist, Mr. Rory. Lindo believes that Waverly does so because she is ashamed of her mother. While Mr. Rory and Waverly discuss her as though she were not there, Lindo wears her "American face"—the face the Americans think is Chinese. But inside she is ashamed, because she is proud of Waverly, but Waverly is not proud of her.

When Mr. Rory notes that Lindo and Waverly resemble one another, Lindo smiles her true smile, wearing her "Chinese face." When Mr. Rory hurries away, Lindo ponders the resemblance in the mirror, thinking about the internal qualities that both women also share. She remembers seeing herself and her own mother back in China, comparing their features then. Her mother told her that she could read her fortune in her face. She had told Lindo that she was fortunate to have a straight nose, because a girl with a bent nose is "bound for misfortune . . . always following the wrong things, the wrong people, the worst luck."

Lindo talks about the difficulties of keeping one's "Chinese face" in America. When she first came to San Francisco, she worked in a fortune-cookie factory, where she met An-mei Hsu. An-mei introduced her to Tin Jong, who would become Lindo's husband. While pregnant with Waverly, Lindo bumped her nose on the bus, making it crooked. She suspects that the crooked nose damaged her thinking, for when Waverly was born, Lindo saw how closely she resembled her and suddenly feared that Waverly's life path would resemble her own. She thus named her Waverly, after the street they lived on, to let her know that America, San Francisco in particular, was where she belonged. She knew that by naming her daughter after their street, she was taking the first step in making her wholly American, and thus alienating her daughter from herself.

In the beauty parlor mirror, Lindo notices that Waverly's nose is crooked like her own, even though Lindo's nose is crooked due to an accident, not her genes. Lindo urges her daughter to get cosmetic surgery, but Waverly laughs because she is pleased to share this feature with Lindo. She says she thinks it makes them look "devious": people know they are two-faced, but they cannot always tell what they are thinking. Lindo thinks about the two faces both women share, and wonders which is American and which is Chinese. When Lindo visited China, she wore Chinese clothing and used local currency, but people still knew that she was an American—she wonders what she has lost.

### SUMMARY—JING-MEI WOO: "A PAIR OF TICKETS"

In the final story of *The Joy Luck Club*, Jing-mei discusses her trip to China to meet her half-sisters, and she finishes the story of her mother's life. When Jing-mei was a teenager, although she knew she looked Chinese, she denied that she possessed any inner, essential Chinese nature below the surface. Suyuan had insisted that once one is born Chinese, one cannot help but feel and think Chinese. Now that she is in China for the first time, Jing-mei feels that there was truth in her mother's assertions—something in her does feel at home in China. Yet, she realizes that she has never known precisely what it means to be Chinese.

Jing-mei now thinks back to the origins of her trip. Not wanting to deceive or disappoint her sisters Chwun Yu and Chwun Hwa, she persuaded Lindo Jong to write to them about their mother's death. Jing-mei and her sisters are the only known living relatives of Suyuan, as Suyuan's entire family died when a Japanese bomb landed on their house, killing several generations in an instant.

Arriving at customs, Jing-mei and her father, Canning Woo, are greeted by her father's aunt, to whom they had previously sent photographs of themselves. Other relatives soon appear to greet the American visitors. Driving to the hotel in a taxi, Jing-mei marvels at the differences between China and America, and she is amazed that the luxurious Hyatt they are staying in costs only thirty-four dollars a night. Although Jing-mei has been envisioning her first real Chinese meal to be a several-course banquet, the relatives wish to stay with them in their hotel for the night and decide to order room service: hamburgers, french fries, and apple pie.

During the night, Jing-mei awakes to hear her father and great-aunt talking: her father is telling his aunt the story of Suyuan and her twin daughters. The aunt then falls asleep, and Jing-mei asks her father about the meanings of the names of her sisters, her mother, and herself. She then asks her father why Suyuan abandoned the twins so long ago. Canning begins to tell her mother's story in English, but Jing-mei interrupts him and asks that he speak in Chinese. Her father then begins the story.

Suyuan had walked to the point of exhaustion, feeling the beginning of dysentery in her stomach. Lying down by the side of the road with the twins, she knew she could not watch them die with her. She begged other passing refugees to take her babies, but to no avail. Finally, she tore open the lining of her dress, where she had stashed her mother's ancient jewels, and stuffed the jewelry into the shirt of one baby, slipping money under the shirt of the other. Taking out photographs of her family and herself, she wrote on the back of each the names of the twins and requested that the rescuer care for the babies with the valuables provided, and, once it was safe to travel, bring them to her address in Shanghai. She stumbled away crying, but soon collapsed. When she regained consciousness, she was in a truck with other sick people and an American missionary. Arriving in Chungking, she learned that her husband had died two weeks before. She and Jing-mei's father met in the hospital, where he had come to be treated for an injury sustained in the Japanese invasions.

Jing-mei's father has since learned that the twins were found by two Muslim peasants, Mei Ching and Mei Han, who lived in a stone cave, hidden from the ravages of the war. By the time they found an educated person to decipher Suyuan's message, they could not bear to part with the twins, whom they had grown to love as their own. Finally, when Mei Han died, Mei Ching decided to take the twins to the address in Shanghai that Suyuan had named. She told her adopted daughters what she knew of their past and their true names, and hoped that she might serve as their nurse in their new home. But the area Suyuan had indicated had been transformed. The year was 1952, five years after Suyuan and Canning had left China, and seven years after the two had visited the address themselves, in hopes of finding the twins there.

For years after coming to America, Suyuan wrote secretly to friends in China in an attempt to find the girls. Only after Suyuan's death did an old schoolmate of hers happen to sight the twins in a department store, recognizing them as if in a dream, identical and resembling Suyuan in her youth. Canning suspects that Suyuan's spirit guided her friend.

As Jing-mei and Canning go to the airport to fly to Shanghai, Jing-mei worries about how to tell her sisters her mother's story, because she feels she hardly knows it herself. She has sent the twins a photo of herself, and when she gets off the airplane in Shanghai they recognize her instantly. The three embrace, murmuring, "Mama," as if Suyuan were there. At first, Jing-mei doesn't think she can see her mother's features in their faces. After Canning takes a Polaroid photo of the three of them, however, Jing-mei looks into the emerging image to find that the combination of the three sisters' faces clearly evokes Suyuan.

## ANALYSIS

Lindo's story continues to examine the cyclical nature of inheritance, a theme raised in this section's opening parable. Comparing her features with Waverly's in the beauty parlor mirror, Lindo notes that their similar faces bespeak similar joys, pains, fortunes, and faults. Waverly even seems to have inherited the crooked nose that Lindo acquired in an accident; this phenomenon symbolizes the force of legacy between mother and daughter—it transcends mere genetic coding. Yet, at the same time, Lindo laments that she has failed to pass on enough of a Chinese cultural consciousness to her daughter. She thinks to herself how ridiculous it is that her daughter could "blend in" in China; only her skin and her hair are Chinese, she thinks, and "inside—she is all American-made . . . It's my fault she is this way. I wanted my children to have the best combination: American circumstances and Chinese character. How could I know these two things do not mix?" She fears that in allowing her daughter to become too American, she has created a divide between Waverly and herself, allowing her daughter to become ashamed of her own mother.

Waverly rejects her mother's understanding of the implications of a crooked nose and teaches her mother that some symbols can have multiple interpretations. Lindo was taught that a crooked nose signifies misfortune and bad judgment, but Waverly thinks it is a positive trait. Her comment that both she and her mother are "devious" and "two-faced" forces Lindo to reevaluate the extent to which American culture has been instilled in her. She has noted her "Chinese" face and her "American" face. But while she considers her American face her insincere face, not the face of her real self, she remembers how the people in China instantly identified her as an American during her trip there. Her American face is not just a protective cover for her Chinese face; it has become part of her identity as an immigrant. Wondering what she has lost or gained by this integration, she resolves to ask Waverly her opinion, to seek the wisdom of her daughter and learn from her in this matter.

Like Lindo, Jing-mei learns a lesson about the nature of Chinese American identity. Jing-mei wanted to reject her Chinese identity in her adolescence because she wanted to be absolutely American. Now that she is traveling to China to meet her sisters for the first time, she worries that she is not Chinese enough. It is not only the language barrier she fears, but also the cultural one. She fears that she did not appreciate her mother enough, while her sisters, who will now never know Suyuan as adults, have honored Suyuan in their hearts for all these years.

Yet Jing-mei also goes further than Lindo in contemplating the nature of a double identity. Lindo feels uncomfortable in her recognition that American culture has left an indelible trace on her. She fears that she has lost a certain purity or honesty of self. In contrast, Jing-mei joyfully comes to recognize the Chinese heritage that lies deep within herself; she happily perceives that the American culture she has embraced for so long does not preempt a Chinese consciousness as well. Seeing her sisters for the first time makes her realize that her identity need not be "proven" to anyone, for it is innate.

It is interesting to note an apparent plot discrepancy. In his description of the discovery of the twins, Canning voices his belief that Suyuan's spirit guided her friend to discover her daughters. However, in the first section of the book, the members of the Joy Luck Club told Jing-mei that Suyuan had located her daughters' address before she died. They mention that she was trying to work up the courage to tell Canning, so it is possible that she never did tell him. It is nevertheless strange that Canning believes the first news of the twins to have come from one of Suyuan's schoolmates after her death, when Lindo, An-mei, and Ying-ying had actually written to the daughters with the address Suyuan had obtained.

In the final paragraphs of the book, when Jing-mei sees that the three sisters together resemble Suyuan, the novel comes to its true conclusion. The real challenge for Jing-mei has been not to find these long-lost sisters, but to find her inner Chinese identity, and to use that as a bridge to her mother. In finding her sisters, Jing-mei accomplishes both; and her success serves as a hopeful example for the other characters in the book, as they continue to struggle for closer mother-daughter bonds despite gaps in age, language, and culture.

SUMMARY & ANALYSIS

# IMPORTANT QUOTATIONS EXPLAINED

1.  "What will I say? What can I tell them about my mother? I don't know anything. . . ." The aunties are looking at me as if I had become crazy right before their eyes. . . . And then it occurs to me. They are frightened. In me, they see their own daughters, just as ignorant. . . . They see daughters who grow impatient when their mothers talk in Chinese . . . who will bear grandchildren born without any connecting hope passed from generation to generation.

This quote, which is found at the end of the book's first story, "The Joy Luck Club," establishes some of the central themes of the novel. The passage establishes Jing-mei Woo as a representative of the book's younger generation, the American-born daughters who feel largely out of touch with their Chinese identities and with their Chinese mothers. As Jing-mei acknowledges this, she also shows a deep sympathy with the older generation. She understands their fears about their daughters, their distress at the idea that their hopes and dreams may not survive them in these modern American women for whom so many of the old values no longer have meaning.

However, even while Jing-mei perceives the mother-daughter gap from both sides, this double perception ultimately serves not to accentuate the gap, but to bridge it. Throughout the novel, Jing-mei provides the connecting voice between the generations. She tells both the story of an American-born daughter longing for independence and the story of her mother, who fought hard to give her daughters the freedoms that she never had. Thus, by the last chapter of the book, Jing-mei will come to represent a figure of hope for both generations, that they might understand each other better than they had thought, that they might share in a dialogue of love that often transcends linguistic and cultural barriers.

2.    I . . . looked in the mirror. . . . I was strong. I was pure. I had
      genuine thoughts inside that no one could see, that no one
      could ever take away from me. I was like the wind. . . . And
      then I draped the large embroidered red scarf over my face
      and covered these thoughts up. But underneath the scarf I
      still knew who I was. I made a promise to myself: I would
      always remember my parents' wishes, but I would never
      forget myself.

In this quotation, which is from Lindo Jong's narrative "The Red
Candle," Lindo introduces what will become an important link
between herself and her daughter Waverly. Here she narrates how
she first came to recognize her inner invisible strength, a strength
that her daughter will inherit and come to use in her chess matches.

This strength gives Lindo the power to endure the hardships that a
restrictive and patriarchal society forces upon her. She stares into the
mirror as she prepares for her arranged marriage to a man she does not
love, knowing that to flee the marriage would be to go back on her parents' promise to her husband's family. Yet she also makes a promise to
herself, which she determines to honor with equal devotion.

Lindo's lesson in balancing duty to one's parents and duty to oneself also links her to her own daughter, and to all of the daughters in
the book, who must learn to revere their heritage and their elders
without becoming passive, without giving up their own desires and
aspirations. While the struggle for this balance often alienates mothers and daughters, it also brings them closer together, for all of them
have faced this challenge at some point in their lives, whether or not
the mothers choose to recollect it.

The central event in this passage—Lindo's recognition of her
value and her subsequent covering of it with her scarf—symbolizes
another lesson in balance. She learns to listen to her own heart and
maintain her strength even as she hides these away beneath the
scarf. She knows that sometimes the strongest force is a hidden one.
Although this gesture of concealment can also easily become a gesture of passivity, Lindo escapes the passivity that characterizes so
many of the other female characters in *The Joy Luck Club* because
she knows when to expose what she hides.

3. "A mother is best. A mother knows what is inside you," she said. . . . "A psyche-atricks will only make you hulihudu, make you see heimongmong." Back home, I thought about what she said. . . . [These] were words I had never thought about in English terms. I suppose the closest in meaning would be "confused" and "dark fog." But really, the words mean much more than that. Maybe they can't be easily translated because they refer to a sensation that only Chinese people have. . . .

This quotation is from Rose Hsu Jordan's story "Without Wood." Rose and her mother An-mei sit in church and speak about Rose's visits to the psychiatrist. Challenging her daughter's adherence to what she feels is an odd Western convention, An-mei asks Rose why she feels she must tell a psychiatrist—a complete stranger—about her marital woes, when she refuses to confide in her mother about them.

Linguistic barriers between Chinese and American cultures are especially prominent in this section of the novel, "American Translation." The passage highlights linguistic discrepancy twice. In the first instance, An-mei appears unable to pronounce "psychiatrist." Yet her mispronunciation may also be deliberate: by calling the doctor a "psyche-atricks," she may be deviously disparaging him as someone who plays tricks on the psyche—a quack not to be trusted. The second illustration of language barriers arises in Rose's own meditations on the Chinese words her mother has used. She struggles to explain them and then wonders whether they can be "translated" into English at all. While one might find substitutes for them in English, she doubts whether the true feeling they connote can be felt by a non-Chinese person. The question then becomes whether these problems of translation inevitably alienate immigrant mothers from their American-born daughters, leading to the situation that An-mei complains of: a situation in which mother and daughter are unable to confide in each other or discuss their inner experiences with one another—in which they must go to strangers for help and support.

QUOTATIONS

4.  Her wisdom is like a bottomless pond. You throw stones in
    and they sink into the darkness and dissolve. Her eyes
    looking back do not reflect anything. I think this to myself
    even though I love my daughter. She and I have shared the
    same body. . . . But when she was born, she sprang from me
    like a slippery fish, and has been swimming away ever since.
    All her life, I have watched her as though from another
    shore. And now I must tell her everything about my past. It
    is the only way to . . . pull her to where she can be saved.

This quotation comes from the beginning of Ying-ying St. Clair's second narrative, "Waiting Between the Trees." Seeing her daughter Lena in a painful marriage, Ying-ying resents her daughter's stubborn refusal to learn from her the Chinese ways of thinking, which Ying-ying regards as wiser than the American ways. Yet she also acknowledges the extent to which her own passivity has led to her daughter's failure to stand up for herself in a dysfunctional marriage. Thus, she knows that the only way to save her daughter is to tell her story, the story of how her submission to fate and other people's wills led to discontent and even agony.

The imagery here creates an especially potent effect and resonates throughout the novel. Although Ying-ying thinks of herself and her daughter as having shared the same body, as being of the same flesh, she also sees Lena as having sprung away like a slippery fish that now exists on a distant shore. Significantly, while many of the mother-daughter pairs view themselves as reflections of one another, Ying-ying looks into Lena's eyes and sees not her reflection but a "bottomless pond." What joins the women—their mutual passivity—is also what divides them.

Ying-ying's notion that the telling of a story can "save" her daughter is not unique in *The Joy Luck Club*. Throughout the book, the mothers insist on the importance of stories not only in guiding their daughters and protecting them from pain, but also in preserving their own memories and hopes, keeping their culture alive.

5.    . . . I wanted my children to have the best combination: American circumstances and Chinese character. How could I know these two things do not mix? I taught [my daughter] how American circumstances work. If you are born poor here, it's no lasting shame. . . . In America, nobody says you have to keep the circumstances somebody else gives you. She learned these things, but I couldn't teach her about Chinese character . . . How not to show your own thoughts, to put your feelings behind your face so you can take advantage of hidden opportunities. . . . Why Chinese thinking is best.

In this passage from "Double Face," Lindo Jong questions the feasibility of the mixed cultural identity she once wished for her daughter. She fears that Chinese identity has come to constitute merely Waverly's exterior, while American identity dominates her interior self. Lindo blames herself for Waverly's lopsided duality.

Yet, from Waverly's own narrative, we know that Lindo's fears are not entirely justified: Waverly exhibits a deep respect and concern for her Chinese identity. Waverly attributes much of her early talent in chess to her mother's lessons in how "not to show [her] thoughts," and she seems to have brought this skill to her adulthood.

Just as Lindo's fears are exaggerated, her descriptions of the American and Chinese ways of life also appear idealized: she seems to believe somewhat naively in the "American Dream," the notion of equal opportunity for all. At the same time, she describes Chinese thinking as "best" and speaks of the Chinese values of obedience and modesty as if they were universally ascribed to in China.

Thus, when Lindo fears that the American and Chinese cultures cannot mix, she is contemplating the combination of two extremes. In reality, each identity is itself mixed: just as the American culture is not wholly about autonomy and liberty, the Chinese culture is not wholly about passivity, obedience, and self-restraint. Nonetheless, the challenge of finding a way to combine aspects of both into one's own unique personality is a challenge faced not only by Waverly, but all of the novel's daughter characters—even, to some extent, by the mother characters, as they become increasingly accustomed to their lives in the United States.

# KEY FACTS

FULL TITLE
*The Joy Luck Club*

AUTHOR
Amy Tan

TYPE OF WORK
Novel

GENRE
Postmodern novel; short story collection

LANGUAGE
English with occasional Mandarin and Cantonese words
and accents

TIME AND PLACE WRITTEN
1985–1989, San Francisco

DATE OF FIRST PUBLICATION
1989

PUBLISHER
G. P. Putnam's Sons

NARRATOR
*The Joy Luck Club* features seven narrators: Jing-mei Woo (who
also tells her mother Suyuan Woo's story); Lena and Ying-ying
St. Clair; An-mei Hsu and Rose Hsu Jordan; and Lindo and
Waverly Jong.

POINT OF VIEW
Point of view in *The Joy Luck Club* shifts from narrator to
narrator. Each narrates in the first person, and sometimes an
event is narrated twice so that we get more than one
perspective—frequently a mother's and a daughter's. The
narrators are highly subjective and tend to focus mostly on their
own feelings.

TONE
Bemused; sorrowful,;speculative; respectful

TENSE

Tense in the novel shifts from past to present as each character reflects on her past and relates it to her present life.

SETTING (TIME)

The novel's events take place within four general time frames: the childhood years of the mother narrators in China; the youthful adult years of the mothers around the time of their immigration to America; the childhood years of the daughter narrators in the United States; and the youthful adult years of the daughters as they interact with their aging mothers. The four time frames span the 1920s–1930s, the 1940s–1950s, the 1960s, and the 1980s, respectively.

SETTING (PLACE)

All of the mother characters' childhood memories take place in China; their youthful memories take place either in China prior to emigration or in San Francisco or Oakland after coming to America. Their American-born daughters remember events that have taken place only in San Francisco or Oakland, although Jing-mei travels to China at the end of the novel.

PROTAGONIST

Each of the narrators serves as protagonist in her own stories, but Jing-mei, because she tells two more stories than each of the other characters, could be said to be the main character.

MAJOR CONFLICT

The Chinese mothers strive to instill their American-born daughters with an understanding of their heritage, yet also attempt to save them the pain they felt as girls growing up in China. The daughters, on the other hand, often see their mothers' attempts at guidance as a form of hypercritical meddling, or as a failure to understand American culture. The daughters thus respond by attempting to further their mothers' assimilation. Both the mothers and the daughters struggle with issues of identity: the mothers try to reconcile their Chinese pasts with their American presents; the daughters attempt to find a balance between independence and loyalty to their heritage.

RISING ACTION

Having located the long-lost twin daughters of their friend Suyuan, the members of the Joy Luck Club want for these grown

Chinese daughters to know their emigrant mother's story. They give money to Suyuan's younger, American-born daughter, Jing-mei, so that she may buy a plane ticket to China and narrate to her half-sisters her mother's tale. Jing-mei fears that she doesn't know enough about her mother to tell her story, but this fear, once expressed, prompts her quest for understanding, also sparking similar quests among the three other women and their three daughters.

CLIMAX

It is difficult to pin down a single climax in the book, as it is composed of interwoven narratives. However, insofar as Jing-mei's narrative is representative of the other characters' situations, the climax of her story may be said to be her trip to China, which serves in many ways as a test of how "Chinese" Jing-mei feels, of whether she in fact knows her mother well enough to tell her story and carry out her dreams. These issues are also at stake in all of the other characters' stories; thus, by embarking on her trip to China and receiving her first impressions, Jing-mei is drawing all of the stories' tensions to a head.

FALLING ACTION

Insofar as Jing-mei's trip to China can be said to be the book's climax, the novel's falling action consists in her realization that she has passed the "test" that the trip constituted. Having journeyed through China for a few days and having met her sisters for only a few minutes, Jing-mei realizes that, deep down, some part of her is in fact Chinese, and that even though she may not think she looks like her sisters or that her sisters look like her mother, the three of the sisters together resemble Suyuan: the sisters will help Jing-mei to come to know parts of her mother that she never before understood, and thus help her to tell Suyuan's story. In this last scene of the book, Jing-mei successfully creates a bridge between two countries, two generations, and two cultures.

THEMES

The challenges of cultural translation; the power of storytelling; the problem of immigrant identity

MOTIFS

Control over one's own destiny; sexism; sacrifices for love

SYMBOLS
Suyuan's pendant; Lena's vase; Lindo's red candle

FORESHADOWING
*The Joy Luck Club*'s realism precludes the use of much foreshadowing. However, because the characters are mother-daughter pairs, a number of the challenges faced by the mothers come to be repeated in some form in their daughters' lives. Many of the mothers' personal strengths and weaknesses are reflected in their daughters, and they struggle with the same issues of obedience versus autonomy, passivity versus assertiveness, whether in relationships with men or other women.

# Study Questions & Essay Topics

## Study Questions

1. *Throughout* The Joy Luck Club, *characters think and communicate using stories. Why might they choose to use stories instead of direct statements? As stories seem a less efficient way of relaying information, do the characters show stories to have some power that normal speech lacks?*

Stories as communication prove especially powerful in *The Joy Luck Club* because of the cultural barriers that stand between the storytellers, often the mothers in the book, and their audience, usually the daughter characters. Because the mothers have had experiences in China that their American-born daughters find hard to understand, they fear that speaking directly of the lessons they have learned might only alienate their daughters.

For example, Ying-ying St. Clair knew many hardships in China. She married a man who was unfaithful and aborted her unborn baby out of her resulting rage. From these experiences, she has concluded that life is full of pain. Yet her daughter Lena might not understand her mother's sufferings. Marrying in one's teenage years is rarely done in America; Chinese culture might view differently the shame of infidelity or the morality of abortion. Thus, to convey to her daughter her perception of the emotional dangers that the world contains, Ying-ying tells Lena a story. She narrates Lena's great-grandfather's encounter with the ghost of a beggar, who pulled the man through the wall to the land of the dead. By telling Lena this story, Ying-ying graphically conveys her sense of fear. Because the story is so simple, it functions more universally than Ying-ying's own. By expressing herself through stories, she communicates to her daughter on a deeper, almost subliminal level, sidestepping the generational and cultural gaps between them. In this way, Ying-ying hopes to make Lena understand and *feel* her fear in a way that the direct restatement of her past might not allow her to do.

2.   *Most of the female characters in* THE JOY LUCK CLUB
     *struggle with oppressive societal structures, often in the
     form of patriarchy and attendant sexism. But in
     America as well, the women characters fall victim to
     sexist structures. Many of the characters respond to this
     suppression simply by becoming passive, silent, and
     indecisive. What alternatives might the characters have?
     Does the book suggest methods by which a woman can
     become powerful? What are the positive and negative
     aspects of these methods?*

The book offers two particularly conspicuous exceptions to its
series of passive women: Lindo's mother-in-law, Taitai, and the Second Wife of Wu Tsing, the man to whom An-mei's mother is a concubine. Taitai represents a tyrannical power: she confines Lindo to
her bed and abuses her in order to get the grandchild she wants. Second Wife manifests a more underhanded cruelty. Deceptive and
manipulative, she banks on her husband's fear of ghosts by faking
suicides so that he will give her what she wants, and she traps An-
mei's mother into marrying Wu Tsing in the first place, wanting to
fulfill his wish for heirs without losing her authority. Both of these
women find ways of asserting themselves within a society that affords
women little power. Yet they manage to do so only by repeating the
very structures of oppression under which they have suffered.

Lindo Jong and her daughter Waverly represent a different kind
of strength: the ability to assert invisible force, keeping silent until
the right moment. Lindo manifests this power in the trick she
plays on Taitai: Lindo takes advantage of a few coincidences to con-
vince Taitai that her marriage to Taitai's son is ill-fated, and that a
secretly imperially born servant girl is carrying the "spiritual" heir
of her husband. Waverly shows the same strength in her successes
with chess: she waits for her opponents to make a weak move, and
then she makes a surprise attack. Nevertheless, while Lindo and
Waverly find in this "invisible strength" a method of gaining power
for themselves and succeeding in a male-dominated world—or a
male-dominated game, such as chess—the method still relies on a
certain passivity. One must depend on the false move of the opponent, on a servant girl's chance impregnation by a deliveryman. Ultimately, the tactic lacks a certain sense of initiative.

In the end, then, passivity remains a persistent problem for the
characters in *The Joy Luck Club*. If they are to avoid being cruel,

they sacrifice power and autonomy. This bind appears to arise at least partially from the patriarchal structures in which these women are living. However, the text does seem to suggest a possible antidote to submissiveness and compliance, a possible means of asserting oneself: the human will. Especially in the narratives of An-mei and Rose, we encounter the viewpoint that one's "assigned destiny" is in fact a matter of will. An-mei urges her daughter Rose to try to save her marriage, saying that one's "fate" consists in being "destined" to struggle. This sense of will does not lead to oppression: it is a persistence to fight against all odds, but not to trample upon others.

The book emphasizes the importance of will not only in the Hsu family's stories, but also more subtly in the other narratives. We recall Jing-mei's realization that she may have found a sense of accomplishment in playing the piano if only she had tried, had put her spirit into it. Will becomes a way not only of achieving one's desires but of achieving those desires in the face of hardship and oppression, in the face of hostile and controlling external forces.

QUESTIONS & ESSAYS

# Suggested Essay Topics

1. Jing-mei fears that she cannot tell Suyuan's story to her half-sisters because she feels that she did not know her mother well enough. Considering her doubts, what is symbolically significant about her agreement to fill Suyuan's place in the Joy Luck Club? What hints do we receive over the course of the book that her fears may be unfounded?

2. Consider some of the cyclical elements in the narratives of THE JOY LUCK CLUB. What are some possible reasons for the cyclical nature of the novel?

3. When Jing-mei tells the story of her childhood conflict with Suyuan over piano lessons, how does her perspective of herself and of her relationship with Suyuan change? How does their conflict represent the conflicts between the other mothers and daughters in the book?

4. How are the daughters in JOY LUCK CLUB American "translations" of their mothers?

5. Over the course of JOY LUCK CLUB, the mothers find themselves learning as much from their daughters as their daughters are learning from them. Discuss what lessons the mothers might have to learn from their daughters. How might the very activity of narrating their stories lead them not just to the sharing of insights but the discovery of new ones?

# REVIEW & RESOURCES

## QUIZ

1.  What game do the members of the Joy Luck Club play?

    A.  Poker
    B.  Chess
    C.  Joy Luck Rummy
    D.  Mahjong

2.  How did An-mei Hsu receive the scar on her neck?

    A.  She was burned by hot soup
    B.  She scraped it by falling into a garden pond
    C.  She got into a fight with her brother
    D.  Her mother ripped a pearl necklace from her neck in order to show her that the "pearls" were in fact glass

3.  How does the red candle predict the success of Lindo and Tyan-yu's marriage?

    A.  If Lindo is unable to blow out the flame, then she will have one love affair outside her marriage
    B.  The number of wax drops that the candle leaves on the tablecloth represents the number of children that Lindo will bear her husband
    C.  If it burns from both ends without going out, it will presage a happy marriage
    D.  The candle will be timed: for each hour it burns, the couple will enjoy a decade of conjugal life

4.     What happens to the candle?

    A.     Lindo blows it out, but the servant lights it again out of fear that she will be punished for negligence

    B.     It burns to the end without going out, symbolizing that Lindo and her husband will have a happy and faithful marriage

    C.     It topples over and starts a fire

    D.     Lindo steals and hides it in order to prevent the marriage

5.     What does Ying-ying's Amah teach her that girls should do?

    A.     They should assert their autonomy and strength despite the pressures of a patriarchal society

    B.     They should try to learn all that they can about the world

    C.     They should never ask questions or make requests, but only listen

    D.     They should learn to dance, play instruments, and recite poetry in order to find good husbands

6.     What is the source of Waverly's first chess set?

    A.     She buys it at a shop in Chinatown

    B.     Her brother receives it as a gift at a church Christmas party

    C.     She receives it as a gift from the men who play chess in the park

    D.     Her mother gives it to her in hopes of awaking an inner prodigy

7.     What does Ying-ying say is wrong with the St. Clairs' apartment?

    A.     It is not big enough

    B.     It is not in Chinatown

    C.     It is not balanced

    D.     Its walls are too thin

8. What is the name of Rose Hsu Jordan's youngest brother?

    A. Matthew
    B. Mark
    C. Luke
    D. Bing

9. How do Rose and An-mei return to the beach to look for Rose's drowned brother?

    A. They are escorted in a helicopter
    B. They take the bus, even though, to Rose's knowledge, the buses aren't running that day
    C. An-mei drives them in the family car, even though, to Rose's knowledge, she has never driven before
    D. They walk twenty miles

10. Why doesn't Jing-mei's piano teacher, Mr. Chong, insist that she play the correct notes?

    A. He is deaf
    B. He does not want to hurt Jing-mei's self-esteem
    C. He believes that the wrong notes sound better
    D. He wants Jing-mei to fail miserably at her recital

11. What does Ying-ying say when Lena fails to eat every last grain of rice in her bowl?

    A. She reminds Lena about the starving children in Africa
    B. She tells Lena she cannot have dessert
    C. She tells Lena to go to her room
    D. She tells Lena that every grain of rice she fails to eat will become a pock mark on the face of her future husband

12. What gift from Rich does Waverly show to her mother?

    A. An engagement ring
    B. A coffee table he has designed and built
    C. A mink coat
    D. A plane ticket to China

13. What material element does An-mei say is lacking symbolically in Rose's character?

    A. Wind
    B. Wood
    C. Fire
    D. Water

14. What is the name of the pendant that Suyuan gives to Jing-mei?

    A. Her "heart's joy"
    B. Her "life's importance"
    C. Her "inheritance of love"
    D. Her "good luck"

15. What is wrong with one of the crabs that Suyuan and Jing-mei buy for their New Year's dinner?

    A. It is missing a leg
    B. It is too feisty and pinches the women
    C. It is brain damaged
    D. It is too small

16. Why does Suyuan end up not eating any crab at all during the celebration?

    A. She has never liked the taste of crab
    B. She is on a no-seafood diet and decides at the last minute to discard the crabs
    C. Waverly takes the best specimen for her daughter, leaving for Suyuan what she had anticipated would be "extra"—the lamed, "unlucky" crab
    D. She miscounted the crabs

17. What does An-mei's mother tell her to do rather than cry?

    A. Fight to correct that which pains her
    B. Speak openly about her sorrow
    C. Sing a song
    D. Swallow her tears and suppress her grief

18. What is deceptive about the necklace that Second Wife gives to An-mei?

    A. It is gold-painted silver, not real gold
    B. It is glass, not pearl
    C. The jade is newer than it looks
    D. It is stolen

19. What measures does Suyuan take to try to ensure that her twin daughters are returned to her after the war with Japan?

    A. None
    B. She tattoos them with her name
    C. She writes the address of her family home in Shanghai on the backs of family photographs and stuffs the photos into the babies' clothing
    D. She hides them in a cave and memorizes the cave's location

20. What does Jing-mei eat for her first meal in China?

    A. Chop suey
    B. Hamburgers, french fries, and apple pie
    C. A traditional Chinese feast
    D. A simple peasant's meal of plain white rice

21. What distressed Lindo about her recent trip to China?

    A. She found that China was not as beautiful as she had remembered it
    B. She was depressed by what the Communists had done to the country
    C. She found the prices too high
    D. She realized that people could recognize her as an American

REVIEW & RESOURCES

22. What is Ying-ying's first step in trying to make Lena realize the problems with her marriage and do something about them?

    A. She kidnaps Lena and takes her back to their family's apartment

    B. She knocks over the rickety coffee table that Lena's husband had made in his student days, shattering the vase that had been sitting on top of it

    C. She tells Lena to go to a therapist

    D. She yells at Lena's husband in front of her

23. What does An-mei use as a prop to keep her kitchen table from wobbling?

    A. A small statue of a Buddha

    B. A Chinese-English dictionary

    C. A Chinese children's book called *The Twenty-six Malignant Gates*

    D. A white leatherette Bible

24. What does Lindo call Waverly's psychiatrist?

    A. A shrink

    B. A "psyche-atricks"

    C. A quack

    D. Dr. Freud

25. Where does Suyuan meet her husband, Canning?

    A. In a hospital in China

    B. At a fortune-cookie factory in Chinatown

    C. At a church function in San Francisco

    D. On a boat coming to America

**ANSWER KEY:**

1: D; 2: A; 3: C; 4: A; 5: C; 6: B; 7: C; 8: D; 9: C; 10: A; 11: D; 12: C; 13: B; 14: B; 15: A; 16: C; 17: D; 18: B; 19: C; 20: B; 21: D; 22: B; 23: D; 24: B; 25: A

# Suggestions for Further Reading

CHU, PATRICIA P. *Assimilating Asians: Gendered Strategies of Authorship in Asian America.* Durham, North Carolina: Duke University Press, 2000.

HO, WENDY. *In Her Mother's House: The Politics of Asian American Mother-Daughter Writing.* Walnut Creek, California: Alta Mira Press, 1999.

HUNTLEY, E. D. *Amy Tan: A Critical Companion.* Westport, Connecticut: Greenwood Press, 1998.

KRAMER, BARBARA. *Amy Tan.* New York: Enslow Publishers, 1996.

TAN, AMY. *The Bonesetter's Daughter.* New York: Putnam Publishing Group, 2001.

———. *The Hundred Secret Senses.* New York: Vintage Books, 1998.

———. *The Kitchen God's Wife.* New York: Random House, 1993.

# SPARKNOTES™ LITERATURE GUIDES

1984

The Adventures of
  Huckleberry Finn

The Adventures of Tom
  Sawyer

The Aeneid

All Quiet on the
  Western Front

And Then There Were
  None

Angela's Ashes

Animal Farm

Anna Karenina

Anne of Green Gables

Anthem

Antony and Cleopatra

Aristotle's Ethics

As I Lay Dying

As You Like It

Atlas Shrugged

The Awakening

The Autobiography of
  Malcolm X

The Bean Trees

The Bell Jar

Beloved

Beowulf

Billy Budd

Black Boy

Bless Me, Ultima

The Bluest Eye

Brave New World

The Brothers
  Karamazov

The Call of the Wild

Candide

The Canterbury Tales

Catch-22

The Catcher in the Rye

The Chocolate War

The Chosen

Cold Mountain

Cold Sassy Tree

The Color Purple

The Count of Monte
  Cristo

Crime and Punishment

The Crucible

Cry, the Beloved
  Country

Cyrano de Bergerac

David Copperfield

Death of a Salesman

The Death of Socrates

The Diary of a Young
  Girl

A Doll's House

Don Quixote

Dr. Faustus

Dr. Jekyll and Mr. Hyde

Dracula

Dune

East of Eden

Edith Hamilton's
  Mythology

Emma

Ethan Frome

Fahrenheit 451

Fallen Angels

A Farewell to Arms

Farewell to Manzanar

Flowers for Algernon

For Whom the Bell
  Tolls

The Fountainhead

Frankenstein

The Giver

The Glass Menagerie

Gone With the Wind

The Good Earth

The Grapes of Wrath

Great Expectations

The Great Gatsby

Greek Classics

Grendel

Gulliver's Travels

Hamlet

The Handmaid's Tale

Hard Times

Harry Potter and the
  Sorcerer's Stone

Heart of Darkness

Henry IV, Part I

Henry V

Hiroshima

The Hobbit

The House of Seven
  Gables

I Know Why the Caged
  Bird Sings

The Iliad

Inferno

Inherit the Wind

Invisible Man

Jane Eyre

Johnny Tremain

The Joy Luck Club

Julius Caesar

The Jungle

The Killer Angels

King Lear

The Last of the
  Mohicans

Les Miserables

A Lesson Before Dying

The Little Prince

Little Women

Lord of the Flies

The Lord of the Rings

Macbeth

Madame Bovary

A Man for All Seasons

The Mayor of
  Casterbridge

The Merchant of Venice

A Midsummer Night's
  Dream

Moby Dick

Much Ado About
  Nothing

My Antonia

Narrative of the Life of
  Frederick Douglass

Native Son

The New Testament

Night

Notes from
  Underground

The Odyssey

The Oedipus Plays

Of Mice and Men

The Old Man and the
  Sea

The Old Testament

Oliver Twist

The Once and Future
  King

One Day in the Life of
  Ivan Denisovich

One Flew Over the
  Cuckoo's Nest

One Hundred Years of
  Solitude

Othello

Our Town

The Outsiders

Paradise Lost

A Passage to India

The Pearl

The Picture of Dorian
  Gray

Poe's Short Stories

A Portrait of the Artist
  as a Young Man

Pride and Prejudice

The Prince

A Raisin in the Sun

The Red Badge of
  Courage

The Republic

Richard III

Robinson Crusoe

Romeo and Juliet

The Scarlet Letter

A Separate Peace

Silas Marner

Sir Gawain and the
  Green Knight

Slaughterhouse-Five

Snow Falling on Cedars

Song of Solomon

The Sound and the Fury

Steppenwolf

The Stranger

Streetcar Named
  Desire

The Sun Also Rises

A Tale of Two Cities

The Taming of the
  Shrew

The Tempest

Tess of the d'Ubervilles

Their Eyes Were
  Watching God

Things Fall Apart

The Things They
  Carried

To Kill a Mockingbird

To the Lighthouse

Treasure Island

Twelfth Night

Ulysses

Uncle Tom's Cabin

Walden

War and Peace

Wuthering Heights

A Yellow Raft in Blue
  Water